THE LAND BETWEEN THE RIVERS

Thoughts on Time and Place

Todd R. Nelson

CAMDEN, MAINE

Down East Books

Published by Down East Books
An imprint of The Globe Pequot Publishing Group, Inc.
64 South Main Street
Essex, Connecticut 06426
www.globepequot.com
www.downeastbooks.com

Distributed by NATIONAL BOOK NETWORK

ISBN 978-1-68475-216-4 (cloth)
ISBN 978-1-68475-217-1 (e-book)

The paper used in this publication meets the minimum requirements of American National Standard for Information Sciences—Permanence of Paper for Printed Library Materials, ANSI/NISO Z39.48-1992.

For Lesley, *the girl in the red*
Yes, The New Yorker *T-shirt.*

Contents

CONTENTS

CONTENTS

CONTENTS

A Note to the Reader

THESE ARE THE ESSAYS I WRITE after I look out the window and see something in a new way, in a new light, like the pasture gate of the first essay. Or when I take a walk down the road and discover something that wasn't there the day before, or perhaps a new thought about the "same old, same old." Or as I daily revisit all my eras and locations, living in a kind of simultaneity with past experiences, cohort, and influences. Boundaries blur. I am an education writer, a rural writer, a local writer, a transcendental writer like Thoreau, and a writer who stumbles upon a good opening line and allows it to unfurl and lead me on. Some days I scribble down an idea in my little pocket notebook. Other days an opening line will spring to mind as I walk, hastening me home to type it out. The rest of the day will be spent taking dictation from the imagination and word associations it precipitates.

A good Thoreauvian never leaves the house without that pencil and paper. I credit several practitioners from my past—E.B. White, John McPhee; Robert Walker, my high school English teacher; various transcendental poets; and Gramma Stone of "Thrush Hour" and Bradford Woods—who instilled the need to examine things, to listen to one's surroundings, and then to say something. Writing is often this second look, or "taking a line for a walk," as Paul Klee said about drawing. Or it is the gate through which I pass following each opening sentence.

It's in the writing process that I often find out what I truly think about something, or find a further line of thought or feeling than I knew was there; a fresh path. What *do* bears think while hibernating; the mouse living in my woodpile; hummingbirds while away for the winter? What are the memories of a person, place, or thing suggested by a stone wall, the mermaid atop the Christmas tree, my favorite pencil, my typewriters, my bicycles, knives, sweaters; my music memories and devotions; the meaning of a scene recorded in an old family photo—quite an array of investigations.

Yes, many of these essays are rooted in locale. I have been a writer in all our previous settlement locales—Boston, London, Scotland, San Francisco, Chicago, Philadelphia, Maine—and in all my prior school communities, any elementary school being an inexhaustible source of writing topics. That exploration—a "Magellanic voyage"—awaits another book, as does the full family arc. This book is derivative of my days when there are no other exigencies beside putting words on paper. This is my writing practice, as opposed to my educator practice. I suppose, however, it's all fashioned of the same cloth, the same tartan warp and weft. It's in the land between the rivers—see final essay.

I pondered how best to sort or sequence these essays for a reader. There's an attraction to thematic sections or chronology. That would be an artificial coherence, a "foolish consistency." So, I've come up with a blend: a rotation through themes without formal sections. I've organized for a serial topic cadence: taking a line for a walk, observation, family history, my story, reports of nature, music, poetry and sacred objects. They could be further parsed as swinging between inner and outer observations, mirth and metaphysical ideas, and past and present. Now I'm getting foolish. You decide. There's no right order; no sequence of composition. Does "Writing Is a Bear" qualify as a report of nature, or is it observation? Frankly, it's all "taking a line for a walk." And informed by my spirit animal. These are the pieces of writing that I like, that taught me something, perhaps about writing itself, or ushered me into a new perspective. Some of the contents were published as monthly columns. When reassembled here, they are untethered from the calendar or periodical pages. They simply come from the heart. I'll call it the John McPhee rotation.

I am the owl, the bear, the deer—curious, observant, attuned to the sounds of the forest, or the incomer, the guy with the stroller, binoculars, and smartphone; the walker of the morning road. And we all have a heartbeat that we listen to as well. Don't forget the fantasy beasts—unicorn and heffalump, and the wily raccoon in the lifeguard chair. They too inhabit my woods and offer a line to take for a walk. Eight generations of family are also onlookers. Past teachers too. I am fond of the memory of an N. Scott Momaday poetry reading long ago. He began by telling the audience, "I am a bear." He meant it. He looked it. Then he read "The Great Fillmore Street Buffalo Drive." I adopted my spirit animal that day and have pondered that poem many times. And now I live among real bears . . . and a forest of poets.

I will admit, that the first and last essays for this collection are purposefully chosen and placed. There's a story between them. Enter through the actual gate that stands down my road a ways; exit through the palimpsest lands of memory, the land between the rivers—all topics which arrive like the bear of one of these essays. I am a bear. I mean it.

—Todd R. Nelson

Illustration by Ariel Rose Nelson

Many of these essays first appeared in the *Christian Science Monitor*, *Bangor Metro*, *The Bangor Daily News*, *The Ellsworth American*, *Maine Public Radio*, *Philadelphia Inquirer*, *The Grand Island Independent*, *Taproot*, *Portland Press Herald*, *Penobscot Bay Press*, and *The Adams School Parent Newsletter*.

The Gate

I'M HAVING A CONVERSATION with an old pasture gate.

It's become my custom to take a walk down our dirt road each morning, before the sun gets too high, on all but the most inhospitable weather days. The dogs, Betty and Lola, badger me until I put on my socks and shoes and select a hat, then we're off. They have their points of olfactory interest all along the verge of the road—checking on the night's wild things, and the messages left by the other neighborhood dogs—and I enjoy inspecting the fields of the old saltwater farms, being kept open by annual mowing.

Though the farm fields are intact, their cow, horse, or sheep occupants are long gone. Some land is committed to a conservation trust. There are a few barns remaining where they must have sheltered. My front field is the remainder of Kendall Ellis's cow pasture. He was the last farmer. The barn has been converted to a human dwelling. The surrounding fields are kept open. The forest, no doubt, wants them back, alder and poplar leering at the open ground, awaiting their chance at restoring their wooded glory days. One neighbor hasn't mowed their field in a few years and the re-invasion is obvious. Most of New England is like that.

There are a few old family cemeteries along the road full of familiar local names. They've been invaded by the trees and the headstones naming the old farm families are toppled or askew.

The most recent additions were made in the 1940s. No one living on the road now bears these names, though our road does.

Toward the end of my stroll, a couple of gates greet me like stoic sentinels of access to the old pastures, a couple of old farming implements rusting within—a manure spreader, harrow, and hay baler. There are bluebird houses on fence posts and an island of milkweed carefully isolated by mowing—interspecies gestures of care. A few years back, there were still sheep grazing. I miss them. The fields need ruminants. So, when I see the gates each day, I provide the rumination. Would the sheep have considered themselves fenced in? Would I be fenced out to them?

The white wooden gate and fence posts are my standard against which to measure the day's weather: cloud cover, fog, sunshine or gloom, the gates stand stolidly open, attendant, a color scale. Like Frost's mending wall, they start my daily conversation with the bird calls I'm learning to identify, and the shy does and fawns that seem to hide and wait for my arrival. Often, in early summer, there were newborns nesting in the tall grass or lupines nearby. Today the Gray Catbird performed its aria; last week, the Bobolink. I might even hear a distant loon out on the river at the bottom of the field. And for how many generations have these birds nested at this very spot? Did the catbird of 1870 sing the same song as today's?

My little dog must think it weird to stop without any other dwellings near and snap a daily photo for the rest of our far-flung family to check in on the Maine coastal forecast. Today's caption: "Glorious, again," as I looked down the pasture to the oak-rimmed river beyond. Other days it could be "cloud cover like the British Isles," or simply "dreich." "There is no bad weather, only inappropriate clothing," as the Scottish adage goes—always suitable for dreich.

It is my neighbor's gate; his land posted. Hunters are not welcome, and I trespass only with my attention-hunting footprints. There is a back path from my house to an interior field, which I sometimes follow to enjoy the forest solitude—just me and the hermit thrushes, or an occasional startled deer when I manage to approach downwind and our trails intersect. The forest buffers the old cow pasture and the back hayfield. This summer there might be two mowings.

I return to the gate. It is a portal to the past use of the land, through which I imagine a farmer trudging through with a scythe, or a son or daughter herding the cows back to the barn for another milking. Despite the new, modern houses on the road, we still inhabit this former, antique landscape, if not its former use. And a portal to imagination. It is a graphic invitation for sketching or print making and might show up in an illustration by my daughter, the recipient of my daily photos . . . herding images and sketches through the gates—and a last sentence, before I turn and head for home.

Flight Aware

I HEAR SONGBIRDS. But which ones? Overhead, jetliners streak to and from Europe. From which countries? Going to which cities? Both flights are reconnoitering on my smartphone as I walk my country road. My two favorite apps hear the birds and "see" airplanes and will answer my questions, identifying both—much better than the myriad apps that just beguile me with mindless scrolling through a parallel, frivolous virtual universe. I prefer these connections to the real songs and flights going on in my immediate surroundings. No scrolling required.

I open the Merlin app, my favorite. And what a perfect double entendre. It is indeed a wizard. It "listens" to the woodland airwaves and records and identifies even the subtlest tweet, turning the song lines of myriad bird species into a chart of sonic peaks and valleys. It detects more birds than my ears do. The finches alone are astounding. The Gray Catbird was a revelation. Ovenbirds, Red-Wing Blackbirds, Northern Goshawks, owls, and Vireos galore, plus a myriad of warblers, sparrows, and thrushes, my favorites, inhabit my road. Eastern Bluebirds! I await discovery of an actual merlin.

Then I open Flight Aware, the Merlin of air traffic tracking. As jet contrails skein the stratosphere, their sonic trails lagging behind, I touch the winged icon on my phone's screen. Flight paths turn into flight plans, with departure and arrival times, destinations, altitude, and air speed. Flight Aware tells me what's flying overhead in real time, anywhere in the world.

The song of a Boeing 747 battling headwinds, from Paris to New York, is no great listening joy. But I like seeing the great migratory arcs across our skies. There's a romance to imagining hundreds of passengers admiring the view of Mount Katahdin from 30,000 feet or wondering at Down East Maine's jigsaw coastline. I also hear the variety of languages and accents being spoken above, as the flight crew prepares everyone for landing, customs, and immigration. "Please remain in your seats with the seat belt fastened low and tight across your lap." Won't be long now.

Having left Europe at noon, they could well be landing at noon thanks to the magic of longitudinal time creep, the earth's rotation, and prevailing easterly winds. They are but white lines behind a silver swallow, barely visible, scribing circumpolar routes in three dimensions across the sky, and two dimensions on my phone, streaming over the maritime provinces, down the Bay of Fundy, over Bangor and my coastline, or diverging slightly, vectored for a city farther west. They are a flight number, a departure time, an air speed, an altitude.

Who are the Icelandic Air passengers who left Reykjavik this morning and will spend the night in New York? Or Zurich to JFK—two heavy planes flying like geese, one at the front of the V formation, one slipstreaming. There's London to Tampa; Frankfort to Greenville, South Carolina; Copenhagen to Boston. Chicago to Addis Ababa is a comparatively exotic, and long flight joining the flow from the west. The world flocks above Maine every day. Our green and pleasant forests and mountains are the welcome landfall of American air space for passengers from Heathrow to Dulles. I have been on that plane. My nest is below. I can see my house from my perch up here.

By late afternoon and evening, the Europe-bound flights from east coast airports begin—vesper flights heading for the chaotic murmuration of Boeings and Airbuses over European airspace like starlings. These passengers will land in all the hubs of Europe, according to my app, jetlagged and ready for breakfast and a nap. They'll be home. Or starting a fresh sojourn. I have flown on those planes too.

Birds enjoy a pilot's-eye view and similar navigational aids; follow similar flight corridors returning to their summer haunts from South American-summer haunts. Some glide through Maine on their way farther north, like their human fliers, final destinations several airports distant. I like a rendezvous for morning and evening songs and even detect differences in the bird species perched in my oaks and firs versus the meadow-dwellers down the road. They are site-specific, according to Merlin, each with a local niche to fill with song.

I would join the avian red-eye, below the jets but still soaring. Sure, I might ride the jet streams for a long-haul route, but I'd also swoop down and inspect my overflight *terroir* from treetop altitude—like the recent Evening Grosbeaks that pillaged my feeder for breakfast, and a weather respite on some grand tour. They were way off course and did not speak Chickadee or Crow, nor request landing permission. They gorged, then departed to their sky-blue highway as quickly as they had arrived—refueled, but not before being identified with my bird flight-aware. I hope they landed safely. But where? Reykjavik perhaps? What's for breakfast, I wonder? Sometimes life imitates an M.C. Escher drawing.

The Sound
of Writing

120 words a minute. . . like a rainstorm on a sheet metal roof.

—Derek

IT SOUNDED LIKE THUNDER, the percussive strokes my father's fingers made on his manual Royal typewriter. It is my earliest emblem of written language and a persistent mnemonic for Dad's verbal gifts. His typewriter was a word engine: a gleaming black mechanism, an industrial factory of printing, hammering letters directly onto paper winding down below its shiny hood where the levers, rods, connecting pulleys, and metal type lurk. It had a hood like a 1955 Buick and the innards of a knitting machine or diesel power plant.

As Dad wrote newspaper stories or worked on his books at night, the gooseneck lamp arching over the keyboard, soft light seemed to pool around his concentration. I recall the poise of his hands above the home keys, attending the next flurry of prose. As I listened from my bed, the sound of those keys striking paper wafted upstairs to my room. The cadence of his certain thoughts punctuated summer twilights. It melded with the sprinklers and cicadas outside, every ten or fifteen words the typewriter's little bell sending the carriage zippering back to the left to drag a new line across the page from the margin. Four bar rest: the non-sound of pondering, then a few phrases murmured under his breath as he tested the sound of the next passage. More thunder, then another pause to backspace and X out the phrase that didn't work. It was typing, not word processing; and typing was music. Keys hit paper, telegraphing letters down into the floorboards through the metal legs of the typewriter table. The Royal had sharps and flats, bass and treble: the staccato space bar; the timpani shift to capital letters; the triangle of the pinky finger making a question mark. It had sixteenth notes of familiar patterns and convenient phrasing: the, is, without, the letters of words which alternated hands allowing greater speed or swinging rhythm to accompany a jaunty thought. Boom, clatter-clatter-clatter, ta-ta-ta-ta-Boom. Ting.

Writing broke the silence of the house at bedtime. Stopping and starting, back and forth, the song of text proceeding out of silence—writing, Dad was explaining through his typing, was something you worked at, tried and retried. It charged my fourth-grade storytelling with the effort to be correct, clear, stylish. And I wanted to type—fast. Stories written on a typewriter had authority because they looked real.

His forty-year newspaper career bridged the evolution from lead type to digital layout on the computer and downsizing from broad sheet to tabloid. Efficiency. If I was lucky, a visit to Dad's desk in the newsroom might include a walk down the hall to pick up lead type headlines left over from the prior day's press run, awaiting smelting and a return to the Linotype machine as fresh ingots. This was alchemy: base metal turned to stories on paper by men who typed for a living. I filled my pockets with leaden words.

My father introduced me to his pals in the composing room, typists with eye shades, fingers flashing above a keyboard appended to a machine the size of our furnace and just as hot. I watched in amazement as lead slugs were pounded out and sluiced into place, letters aligning themselves in reverse order line by line, paragraph by paragraph until a whole broad sheet of typeface had been assembled and sent to be positioned in the press. On a good day, visiting after deadline, I might be awarded a slug with my own name in 14-point letters and return to school with a primal artifact of publishing.

My own children have never used a standard typewriter. As they peck their way through book reports, watching their words flicker on the computer monitor, writing is television. No heft. This laptop of mine replaces a whole newsroom and composing room as it lays the illusion of publishing at my fingertips without weighing more than a few paragraphs of the old lead type. Hundreds of fonts reside in its circuitry; any size type; bold, italic, underlined and shadow; even color; justified margins. It is the apotheosis of Gutenberg's revolution. But it has changed the rhetoric of invention: this paragraph has no living history, no record of its deletions or verbal heritage, only a current avatar. Every text file is a palimpsest; writing and editing sleight of hand, magical disappearing acts, as letters and words simply evanesce.

Without music. This is a synthesizer to the Royal's piano, a sterile clicking that transmits words, phrases, and sentences in identical timbre. The reverberant aural power of words, mechanically hammered onto the page with emphatic variations in speed and pressure, is missing. The laptop has no apparent moving parts—all circuitry, all plastic. No inky ribbon; no fingerprints. No Buick hood. No diesel. No percussion. No thunder. To my children, this is typing; this is writing. But I remember the sound of real writing: the engine of my father's words.

Thoreauvians I Have Known

MR. WALKER, MY 12TH GRADE ENGLISH TEACHER, was known for his devotion to Henry David Thoreau. His yearbook quote always came from Thoreau. In 1974, the year I graduated, it was: "For the improvements of ages have had but little influence on the essential laws of man's existence." Mine was, "Gie me ae spark o' Nature's fire, That's a' the learning I desire." Robbie Burns. For Walker, all roads led back to the outlook of Thoreau. We students knew it and always took pleasure in beating him to the punch with an attribution of any deep inner meaning to Thoreau. It's good to have a go-to transcendentalist in your life.

Another English professor I knew, Paul O. Williams, talked of how to *be* a Thoreauvian. For one thing, it meant always being prepared to observe—and to take notes. Like Thoreau, he always had a pencil and notebook at hand, and any walk could be made a Thoreauvian experience. He never knew Mr. Walker, but they would have had much to share on a visit to their Mecca: Walden Pond.

My favorite prose writer, John McPhee, took a deep dive into Thoreau when he wrote about the Native American bark canoe. He and Henry Vaillancourt, of Greenville, New Hampshire, maker of authentic bark canoes, had followed Thoreau's water trail and portages through the Maine woods and Penobscot River watershed using Henry's bark canoes. He chronicled Vaillancourt and their trip in *The Survival of the Bark Canoe*. I'll always be grateful to McPhee for a favorite sentence in which he talks about floating by Umbazooksus stream and enjoying the "silence of a moose intending to appear." That is full of the powers of observation and suggestion of exactly what should, could, would appear. I like the image of McPhee, paddle resting athwart the gunwale, notebook in hand, recording the non-appearing of the potential moose. Very transcendentalist of him.

I managed to get Henry Vaillancourt to visit my school while I was teaching *Bark Canoe*. That school was in Concord, Massachusetts. It's where "God's drop," Walden Pond, is, of course, as well as plenty of other vestiges of Thoreau's life there. It's the epicenter of the American transcendentalist philosopher landscape and society—Emerson, Alcott, et al.—in which Thoreau thrived, even while pretending to keep a slight distance.

E.B. White was a great Thoreauvian and even shared Thoreau's birthday, July 12th. Since White's farm isn't too far away from us, and his observations of life hereabouts stand the test of time, it's his practice of his observations that I take most to heart. "What seemed so wrong to Thoreau," White wrote, "was man's puny spirit and man's strained relationship with nature." White could have written the following sentiments from *Walden*. Man's possessions, Thoreau writes, are "more easily acquired than got rid of," and he cites the Mucclasse Indian annual burn ritual. The village would burn old food and belongings to cleanse and purify, followed by a fresh start. Even the fire on the hearth would be restarted by their high priest.

"I have scarcely heard of a truer sacrament," Thoreau writes, "as the dictionary defines it: 'outward and visible sign of an inward and spiritual grace.' We often forget that resolutions may begin with the motive to be different, new. But to be successful, the reformer must make room." Most New Year's resolutions forget the "make room" part.

White made sure to distinguish between Thoreau and a naturalist: he wasn't. Perhaps his response to the wilderness of Maine clinched that, as McPhee rooted out. Nor was he a complete hermit. For a guy who advocated simplicity and tiny houses, he spent a lot of time in big Main Street houses in Concord. But White appreciated him for being a writer, an observer, a recorder of responses to his surroundings, and reducing life to the essentials that spark joy.

"*Walden* is the only book I own," White wrote in *The New Yorker* in 1953. "Every man, I think, reads one book in his life and this is mine. It is not the best book I ever encountered, perhaps, but it is for me the handiest, and I keep it about me in much the same way one carries a handkerchief—for relief in moments of defluxion or despair."

Finally, we owe our pencil quality to Thoreau's innovative use of clay to improve the New Hampshire plumbago comprising the core of his father's products—better hardness and smear-resistant. He considered himself a civil engineer. Has his improvement of the tool of the ages affected the essential laws of my nature? No doubt. I always pocket a pencil and notebook when I leave the "cabin," ready to jot down my perceptions of anything that might be intending to appear.

Reports of Nature

THE GRAND SHAMAN OF CAMP INDIAN NAME always requested "reports of nature." It came after games of skill and before the word of the week. We, his faithful camper constituents, wrapped in our wool blankets, swatting mosquitoes and itching the crusted lines of tempera paint on our faces, awaited his arrival at dusk for a piece of theater called the Saturday night council fire.

He came from across the lake to our swimming beach standing, arms akimbo, on a plywood platform lashed between two Grumman aluminum canoes like a catamaran, paddled by four athletic, sinewy chiefs in loin cloths, who looked suspiciously like our cabin counselors. The resonant beating of 50-gallon oil drums provided a solemn timbre for his arrival. The drummers had, evidently, listened to a lot of In-a-Gadda-Da-Vida back in their college dorms.

In fulfillment of camp lore, the GS made his way from his home on Mount Chocorua each Saturday night, to the waters of the long, narrow lake, drawn to the beacon of the drums. Once he reached shore, he sternly presided.

The first order of business: command the fire be lit. Much of our anticipation of council fire was seeing exactly how it would be lit. This always took place in a novel manner, often involving an accelerant: a rocket on a wire from the woods, a scuba diver bringing fire invisibly across the lake surface, a junior counselor breathing fire with a war cry. It was the sole job of several head counselors to spend the whole of the intervening week engineering the pyrotechnics using rockets, accelerants, and kerosene. It was worth it. The results were awesome, mysterious, and even terrifying.

The GS never spoke. He used sign language. This was translated by White Bear, his chief of staff. The Grand Shaman had a sign vocabulary like a major-league coach signaling his runner to steal second base on the second pitch, or telling a batter to swing away. His gestures had gravitas as he patiently dispensed wisdom and high expectations for camp conduct and aspiration in field sports, hikes, riflery, archery, canoeing, and sailing. And he inspired observation of the natural world, public speaking, and sharing. He always wanted to know what we had observed on our hiking and canoeing trips that week. "It is time for reports of nature," White Bear would finally announce.

I looked forward to it. Who didn't want to stand, raise an arm, be recognized, and relate an astounding nature-sighting from a week spent on trips, or even walks through the woods and paths down to the lakeside docks. I yearned for the bald eagle, loon, deer, moose, or even (hope of hopes) a bear sighting. I planned my report for the GS around this potential astounding spirit animal evanescence.

Alas, chipmunks and garter snakes tended to dominate reports. The wilder denizens of the forest gave camp Indian Name a wide berth from June to August.

However, Reports of Nature started a lifetime of observation and active perception, my manner of moving through the natural world and paying attention to its signs and wonders. It would change my jaunts through the forest back at my suburban home, across the street and down the path through the white pines to the big pond—a vestigial wilderness full of report potential.

Reports of Nature inaugurated my point of view and observational practice during grander hikes in the White Mountains of New Hampshire, the western mountains of Maine, the Highlands and Cairngorms of Scotland, and eventually our own twenty acres of pine and cedar Maine woods, a perfect coyote and bear habitat. Any brief stroll could yield a footprint, a hawk or turkey feather, or matted snow bed from where the deer herd up at night.

And so it is even today, just looking out the window in anticipation of another visit from my local fox, or the porcupine, or perhaps the doe leading her fawn through our front meadow . . . and someday the elusive, secretive, shy bear that I know is waiting on the forest verge to join this week's reports of nature, I consider the potential for reports of nature. My neighbors all have their reports. Hannah, just had her beehive ransacked by a bear—for a second time. Sylvia and Becky saw one crossing the road in front of their car. One tipped over Goshia's chicken coop. So, I know he's out there.

And granddaughter Freya has been inducted into the order. She has adopted the language and observational mission of detecting and sharing Reports of Nature.

"Opa!" she exclaims over FaceTime. "I have a report of nature!" Turtles on the riverbank, a snake on the road, large-winged birds of any kind, and special flowers follow. She is proud of her information gathering, and sharp eye for natural details. She has become a looker and a watcher. The torch has been passed to a new generation. When her backyard chicken coop gets repopulated, I expect egg production to qualify as reports of nature. I hope to finally learn where eggs come from.

Dear bear, we still have a few days before council fire. Please drop by—a brief visit will suffice. Would a few donuts make it worthwhile? Grand Shaman: I expect to have something to share. Call on me!

'Neath the Cover of October Skies

IT'S AN ANNUAL REUNION. After just a few crisp nights in October, when "the leaves on the trees are falling," and there's a harvest moon foxtrotting among the branches, I am snapped back into the teenage barn dance where I first heard "Moondance" by Van Morrison. "Well it's a marvelous night for a moondance . . . with the stars up above in your eyes . . . the calling of your heartstrings soft and low." It always reinstalls the mood of that first hearing, back "'neath the cover of October skies." Perhaps you know what I'm talking about? It is an ode to autumn as a puckish, ripening midsummer's eve of romance, and that October becomes this October, every October.

My friend Doug was hosting some other high school kids and had been decorating his suburban barn for the occasion. Harvest theme. I remember a few attendees, perhaps a little swing dancing, some refreshments, hay bales, subdued strings of light, the harvest vibe, and cooling temperatures. Was there a moon? Maybe. But "Moondance" is what's etched in memory. It jumpstarted 11th grade. The whole album became a sonic suite of my adventurous high school years. It invited a romantic mood before there was romance. It would become the soundtrack to future romance, perhaps the litmus test. Certainly, the sponsor and guide. It was for *us*, before there was an *us*. I had yet to discover just whose eyes the stars were up above in.

And after that, there was only one Van. His is not a singing voice, *per se*, more like a tenor sax. And it only requires the first two ascending piano chords of "Moondance" to feel all the old feeling. Like an astral Courtier poet, Van sets the antecedent stage for love and more love. But on the album, you must first hear "And it stoned me," and the story of jumping right in a swimming hole. After "Moondance" it'll be "Crazy Love." The album narrates some of my favorite rural teenage adventures, like skinny dipping in the town reservoir or neighbor's pool. And it anticipates so many later scenes. Come to think of it, there's been a Van album attached to every period of my life.

Moondance became *our* album, our songs. Thirty years later, married with three kids, we saw Van Morrison live in San Francisco. Georgie Fame, Junior Wells, Johnny Witherspoon, and John Lee Hooker were in the all-star backing band. "Moondance" was the song everyone waited for, and even its re-orchestration as an R & B medley seemed perfect. We later bought the recording of the live concert and wore it out in the car CD player.

It appeared in the show in a medley with "Gloria," Van's prior breakout hit with his Ulster bandmates, Them. Every garage band knows its three chords and narrative. "She makes me feel alright." And spelling lesson, second only to R-E-S-P-E-C-T.

Then came *Hymns to the Silence, Enlightenment, The Healing Game,* and a lot of *The Essential Van Morrison*-type albums. Van was there for us, with us, across country, houses, children, jobs, and other adventures—previous, way back, Van awaited. And bands. Every band I've played in had to have some Van in the repertoire, starting with the first band playing "Gloria" down in the wood-paneled basement. Three chords, no bridge, and "Shout it every night."

There are, of course, other album/song reunions invoked by just the right trigger memory. We all stash them deep in our soul of souls, sometimes undetected, dormant, for music is "the food of love," as Duke Orsino puts it. And that line too may be a kind of reunion for us English majors. "Play on. Give me excess of it."

"Moondance" still posits a bower of possibility, of romance, of a jumpy swaying cheek to cheek; a fantabulousness that is rare and ideal—but possible. Love set to music. A dance tune: not a symphony, but a lyric that gets your feet tapping and makes the room swoon. There's only one other dancer in it. All your dreams will come true then. "Shall we make the welkin dance indeed?"

You know how this ends, how Van brings it on home. "Can I just have one more moondance with you . . . in the moonlight . . . on a magic night. . . . Can I . . . just have . . . one more . . . moondance . . . with you . . . my love." Saxophone and flute trill. Fade away. Van the Man out. Never gets old; every time a reunion. I'm back in the Avalon barn; smitten with being smitten; dancing and seventeen; redreaming on a mystic isle of memory and a backward persistence of vision. G-L-O-R-I-A in *excelsis day glo.*

Writing Is a Bear

. . . AS DISCUSSED IN A WRITING CLASS after an example by John McPhee.

You see, even if you don't like to write you have a handy topic: writer's block itself. You could start out with a letter, like John McPhee advises.[1] "Dear Mr. Nelson," you might say, "I do not like to write! I have such a hard time thinking of a topic. This assignment is a total bear." Then you could go on and on saying why, and what it feels like to have no ideas and feel blocked and stymied, whining about how useless it feels to persist. And yet write you must.

"It's like strolling along a path through the woods, minding your own business," you could write, "when you 'round a corner and you startle a bear. He comes thrashing through the bushes to investigate. Now you're also startled." This bear-writing assignment does not like surprises and he's big and hungry because he's fresh out of hibernation. So, he starts moving toward you with a famished look in his eyes. And you must decide, *shall I run for it?* But then you think better of that option since the bear is certainly going to outrun you. *I'll climb a tree!* Silly. Bears are better tree climbers too. Play dead? You're ticklish. Wouldn't last long. And here his big furry self comes, heading straight toward your lunch bag, which his big black nose has detected, licking his lips, and no doubt thinking, *Easy pickings, this one.*

So now you're down to your last option which is to look the bear in the eye and prepare to stand your ground and out-fierce him—and you do—until finally you are toe-to-toe, breathing his hot stinky bear-fresh-from-hibernation breath, thinking, *My, what big teeth you have.* And the bear is thinking, *I am so misunderstood. All I wanted was a morsel of that peanut butter and jelly sandwich that smells so heavenly.* And you wonder, *Perhaps, he would settle for my PBJ sandwich.* So, you pull it out of the bag slowly and offer it on the palm of your hand, and the bear sniffs it and decides that it seems like a very fair deal and involves far less effort than picking your own berries, one by one, or invading a beehive and stealing honey from little buzzing things that sting or hitting bird feeders again. And so the deal is silently struck, and the bear gets lunch and you get your writing assignment done. You take John McPhee's advice and just remove "Dear Mr. Nelson" from the page and retitle it "My Lunch with the Bear.'" Sometimes the bear eats you (or your sandwich), and sometimes you eat the bear (or, the assignment). Way to go.

Waiting for writing to appear is akin to another McPhee wildlife scene, canoeing by Umbazooksus Stream. "We will stop paddling, stop talking, and stay until a moose shows up or the stream freezes. We settle down to wait. Stillness envelops us. It is the stillness of a moose intending to appear."# Awaiting writing inspiration is the stillness of a *bear* intending to appear. It is the stillness of this paragraph intending to be read.

Now you're thinking, *I wonder if that bear has cubs?* Of course it does. Just like this essay will.

NOTES

1. *Draft No. 4* by John McPhee.
\# *The Survival of the Bark Canoe.*

Glasgow Necropolis— Back to the Old Country

June 15, 2011

Tonight I will be on a plane to Glasgow, the city of my ancestors. In two days, my daughter, Ariel Rose Nelson, graduates from Glasgow School of Art. "We" left four generations ago and have been looking back ever since. It's a common enough Scottish story, but it's new each time to the generation that makes the trip. It's also a common enough American story, since we all began somewhere else and millions of us feel this urge to locate our origin. Going back to the remote source of our DNA helps to explain why we're here, and who we *are*.

I'm drawn to the sheer romance. On July 2, 1867, Ariel's great, great, great grandparents, Alexander Nelson, a journeyman joiner, and Jeannie Callum, of 23 Hunter Street, were married by Rev. Woodrow Thompson of St. Luke's Church, Glasgow. Alexander was 24 years old, son of Agnes Punten and James Nelson, plough-man. Jeannie was 23, one of the eight children of James Callum, shoemaker, and Jane Cave. On their honeymoon, she and Alex-ander emigrated to Toronto, eventually settling near Buffalo, New York. And that's about all we knew about "our" departure.

Their son James named his son Robert, who named his son Robert, who named his son Todd, who named his youngest child Ariel. And she decided to go to the old country as a third-year college student to finish her degree in graphic design.

She is the third Nelson to go back to the old country. I was the first. During my own junior year abroad at Stirling University in 1976, my grandfather (the elder of the Roberts) came to Scot-land, his first trip across the pond. Grandfather had instilled in me the modest amount he knew of our Scottish roots. Who were "our people," back beyond living memory? Clan Gunn, of Norse origin, has always been part of the answer. Who and where are the distant relations of our clan? Not sure. But surely there are cousins. Our mission: find family records in the registry house in Edinburgh. We did.

Grandfather and I enjoyed a reunion when we opened a leather-bound ledger and read the page where, in an antique script and fading ink, Alexander and Jeannie's wedding was recorded. Lacking the birth dates or locations to search parish records, we were blocked. Nowadays, from my house here in Philadelphia, I can open the same exact ledger with my com-puter and see the same script and wonder the same thing: are there cousins? Digital reunions won't suffice.

The Callum-Nelsons must have been typical of their social class in 19th century Glasgow. Evidently, Scotland held no promise. It must have required great courage or desperation or both to leave family, friends, and the known world and set out for America by steamship. They never saw their homeland again, though Jeannie's Glasgow accent never faded and, according to grandfather, she still called her childhood friends by name 60 years away from the playmates of her youth. She died in New York in 1934, age 90.

The occasion of my trip to the city of the ancestors has stimulated some energetic research on my part. I was bound and determined to find some Callum or Nelson cousins—and I did. The Callums have dispersed as far as Australia and as near as Nottingham and Glasgow, where cousins still reside. We've exchanged genealogical tidbits and photos. Until just recently, Alexander's family eluded me. Then I located him at age seven in the 1851 Scottish census. There was the family, with the right parental names and siblings, including a younger brother named James.

What's more, I've even found their houses. The census gave me a location, and courtesy of Google Earth I can descend on the wee village of Spott, Dunbartonshire, and see the little stone cottage in which Alexander and his siblings were counted in the census. The row of houses sits amid the fields that James Nelson no doubt plowed. A few more clicks and I found the cottage where he was born, not far away. It seems as if their lives were lived within a fairly circumscribed area—except for the son that up and left for America and started this whole grand arc of family dispersal . . . and return.

So, it's a reunion of sorts: me, grandfather, Jeannie, in memory and desire. No one stays behind in the digital age. If 19th century marriage records traverse cyber space, so can we. If we can't see farther into the past, perhaps we can work from 1867 to the present? I'd like nothing more than to talk with a descendant of the folk that remained in Glasgow, and I now know the name of a Callum cousin with whom I share a great, great, grandfather. We will land in the morning. Wouldn't great-grandmother Jeannie be amazed! A digital reunion simply won't suffice.

Seeing a World in a Grain of Sand

TOM COULD SEE "a world in a grain of sand." An English teacher in addition to being a sand maven, Tom collected sand with a little help from his students. Knowing of his collection, they would return from vacations with small vials of the precious granules from beaches around the country and the world. Tom bottled any contribution and added them to his collection, which eventually incorporated the stuff of beaches from the Atlantic to the Mediterranean and back via the Pacific. I added crucial sand from Scotland missing from his inventory.

I should call him a sand maven. Tom labeled the containers and lined them up in a siliceous color spectrum from white to beige and textures from coarse ground pepper to sugar. But unlike philatelists or lepidopterists or numismatists, Tom's collection left much to the imagination. Thank goodness.

One had to siphon the complementary sounds of surf and seagulls from his Maine vials; the images of sandpipers scurrying ahead of the tide encapsulated in his Sanibel Island vial; the bleak North Sea wind brought to you by imagining sand from Scotland.

Sand is surely the oldest of artifacts. It is the raw material of these ephemeral fantasies, as well as the enduring cathedral window, the inter tidal castle, or more prosaic bricks and mortar. Even a tiny vial of sand can't help but invoke thoughts of palm trees, footprints, bare feet. Sand is always found in nice places and numerous metaphors.

Tom's collection inspired me to keep natural artifacts of my own travels, whether from a leisurely paddle to the island across the river or a jet flight to another country. It's important to bring something back from unfamiliar places. And any walk around the block becomes an investigation of an unfamiliar place.

I started my own collection of sand, but as I rarely found myself on exotic beaches the practice ended with a single jam jar of Malibu's finest. During January in Maine, it induced warm thoughts of surfing and lolling in the sun on the famous beach. But with little chance of growing beyond Malibu, this collection stalled. I passed the grains of bleached surfer dude beach along to a friend as a silly Christmas present. Perhaps it has seeded a collection for him?

I moved up the evolutionary chain from sands to rocks but clung to the shore as the artifact zone. Collections need parameters. When we lived in Chicago, my office in-box brimmed with evocative stones gleaned from remote fields and shores—from Lake Michigan and up and down the east coast.

For instance, the smooth purplish lumps from a friend's pebbled shore in Nahant, Massachusetts always reminded me of our evening spent catching blue fish from the rocks. And there are diverse Maine stones: smooth granite from West Grand Lake, special pebbles with unique tidal carvings from coves on the Penobscot Bay coastline, each a reminder of a canoe trip or beachcombing.

This collection weighed down many a summer suitcase riding the luggage carousel at O'Hare, as we returned home from vacation.

I wised up. I gave away my rock collection to my school colleagues when we moved. Each rock, once an artifact of my days next to bodies of water, became an artifact of friendship, collegiality, and years of rapport.

I switched to driftwood, nature's best found-sculpture. Even a humble branch or cedar stump, salted and sanded over the winter into smooth, writhing shapes, can evoke recollections of time on the shore as well as fantastical projections. Like cloud gazing, finding abstract shapes in driftwood makes art out of happenstance. Driftwood too makes an excellent present. When I gave Paul a particularly exquisite gnarled lump, he saw the dancer in it right away and hung it above his desk to float and jump.

Crow feathers came next. Crows abound in our town, and their feathers drift down daily from their Elm canopy aeries. I pick them out of the grass and add them to the collection can, a large bouquet of delicate, black lift. Last summer I had enough to give a friend fifty feathers, one for each year, for her birthday. Fifty ways of looking at fifty.

I've decided that such collections are different from most and generate different philosophies and practices. They are made to be passed on, in the same manner they arrived, not hoarded nor held for appreciation.

The sand, stones, driftwood, or feathers have arrived by currents of water or air or time, and they move on to their next collector in a similar, abstract current. They become the currency of special tidings, a signifier of connection, a one-of-a-kind artifact of friendship.

Conversations
with My Father

MY FATHER, ROBERT COLBY NELSON, could hold a conversation with anyone. My favorite recollections are of him doing just that. His print, radio, and television journalism career took him to myriad places and stories in 40 years of reporting. He earned a living starting conversations with unlikely people, in unlikely places.

As a correspondent in Chicago, he won an award for covering ward politics. He traveled to the southern states at the height of the civil rights movement, and then years later to Ulster at the height of The Troubles. He had plenty of conversations with famous newsmakers, and with the man in the street and the common people behind the news. He put an intimate, familiar face on the big, seemingly remote stories of several reporting eras. He gave readers the heart of a shared humanity across difficult dividing lines and conflicts. Dad could talk with white men, black men; Protestants, Catholics; the mighty and the downtrodden; rich and poor. Strangers became friends; the untrusting, trusting.

On any given casual outing, Dad struck up conversation. He loved to talk with the London cabbies during our years in

England, learning about The Knowledge of London driving routes, and the day's politics or most recent trade union action.

But two conversations stand out to me: one of the earliest I remember from my youth, and one I know of only through a photograph I found after his passing.

Dad hated fishing. But when I was about nine, he took me fishing not far from his boyhood home in Buffalo. I think he felt a certain duty to indulge my interest, and so we set off with an old rod, hooks, and worms, to sit beside a creek. The fish weren't biting, but the thin slate rocks on the creek bed were worthy of a few hours spent skipping stones while watching the bobber.

The more powerful memory is of Dad's conversation with the unemployed steelworker sitting on the bank nearby, also watching his bobber in the current. The gist of their conversation never made any sense to me. But I see it now as my earliest recollection of Dad's professional voice.

I remember the tone of the men talking, the feeling of the heavy summer air, and a certain slant of light filtering through the trees above. And as with many of Dad's subsequent conversations, I remember the earnest quality of the transaction. Dad was curious about the stranger's story. The steelworker found someone who took a genuine interest in his lot, and he opened up. There was a bridge, and strangeness couldn't persist.

It's not that the journalist in my father was always seeking the story potential in anyone he met, but that he simply saw the truth in everyone's story and wanted to hear it. There was always the possibility of arriving at the point where one could say, "I know you. I see you." Familiarity.

The photo I cherish comes from the 1980s during one of Dad's trips to Russia. He was no doubt fulfilling a longstanding dream of interviewing poet Yevgeny Yevtushenko. Dad studied Russian in high school and college, then got a master's degree in

Soviet studies, preparing himself for the big professional story of his era: the Cold War and Soviet-American relations.

In a later phase of his career, he was a journalist attached to the Kettering Foundation's Dartmouth Conferences and made numerous trips to Russia as a member of high-level discussions and exchanges. I love his photos of visits to St. Petersburg, the Hermitage, and his tales of life in the waning years of the Soviet Union.

But this photo is different. It's a small story. The two men must be at a dacha. There is spring foliage. Dad stands beside Yevtushenko. The poet is holding an apple and obviously in midsentence. He is expounding. Dad has obviously set his camera on a tripod and used the self-timer, then dashed into the frame. He directs his gaze straight into the lens. His expression suggests he is thinking, "How cool is this. I'm standing next to Yevtushenko."

He is midconversation with the poet, with himself, with the audience for the photo . . . with me. And I know the tone of voice that characterized the afternoon of questions and answers, the sharing between the American journalist and the Russian poet, as their stories became real to one another. To Dad, journalism itself was a conversation, and the big story could be as present in the tale of the steelworker as in the expounding of the great poet.

There is, of course, a third conversation to relate, and it's ongoing: my own, with my father, in each opportunity to hear someone's story. I too ask the cabbies, with immense curiosity, where they're from. And whenever I set out to write, I've come to see that it's actually a conversation with my father. Thanks for the conversations, Dad.

My Bookshelves, My Self

I GAZE AFFECTIONATELY at my bookshelves. It's something the Kindle does not offer. It has no dog-eared and yellowed pages showing affection and use. It does not have the tapestry of my reading on full display. The digital book only has a present tense.

My daughter jokes about my proclivity toward never discarding a book. "Dad! When will you ever need all that poetry?" she says scornfully. "You'll never read that book again." She clearly has a recessive gene.

She's right, in the literal sense, however you just never know when a formative book will be needed for reference or mere perusal or simply it's comforting abiding presence on the shelf and talisman of times passed. It is a companion, a visitor from a former time. Glancing through the colorful spines is an emotional re-acquaintance with reading foretold. My books, I am thinking, are a complete geography of personal history, the repository of my miscellany of lives, without even getting into the marginalia or various photos and letters secreted in the pages. I recently rediscovered the high school yearbook photos that my girlfriend and I snapped in a field of milkweed. They were filed in a Sierra Club book of the era. I left them safe where I found them.

One would think, from the eras comprised in my collection, that I had never given a book away. Here is my college English major collection, side by side with my English teaching career collection, beside the books of several childhoods—mine, my parents, my children, my grandchild—and the arc of location and relocation from coast to coast and various stints, stays, and adventures.

It's odd, in an era when most of my books are available in digital format, to think that carting around stacks of paper makes any sense. And yet these are indeed comforting old friends—my back pages of location, development, thinking, ambition, and tender affinities. They are the bookmarks of my life. A bookshelf is not about spatial economy but emotional archives.

Just gazing at them is a reunion with old friends and former selves; a review of a lifetime of reading habits. Books sitting on shelves are silent. Inspected, they talk back. Though they have been boxed and trucked across country and from house to house numerous times and look somewhat the worse for wear, even in their dotage they speak.

Here is the book of London street maps from the early 1970s when our family lived there and I was an American high school student, plucked from American suburbia and free to explore the worldly metropolis. Later came the map books of France, Scotland, regions of the United States, each summoning a pang of longing for their blue highways and meals and local colors.

Here are the childhood books of my parents, artifacts of a century of family reading. I notice my childish scrawl on the title page of *Lone Cowboy*, a favorite of my mother's: *Todd Robert Nelson*. I was in a phase of eschewing my *actual* middle name in favor of my father's.

Here are the college poetry anthologies, waymarks of an English major and path toward teaching and writing. And then a myriad of slender collected, selected, and new poems. My tastes are showing. Each index is annotated; table of contents starred—a running record of what I liked and when. Can I remember why?

Here is the big red collected poems of e.e. cummings, my first personal acquisition, a Christmas present when I was in high school. Next on the shelf: Dylan Thomas, a favorite ever since Mr. Walker's English class. Then Yeats and William Stafford, with Wendell Berry and Philip Booth, once our neighbor in Castine. A few inches further along lie Billy Collins and the poets to whom he introduced me when he was poet laureate: Ron Koertge, Dana Gioia, Louis Jenkins.

The poets of teaching—authors that made a particular point, for a particular class of mine, about "how a poem means" (John Ciardi's phrase), or the music of words, or the taut rhetoric of sense and sensibility (that's the name of an anthology). Richard Wilbur (my copy of his selected poems is signed to my father—they must have met for an interview), Ceslaw Milosc (signed, a gift), and Seamus Heaney. There is no rhyme or reason here, just the mosaic of my understanding and worldview. Wendy Cope, Virginia Hamilton Adair, Charles Simic. Borges. Garcia Lorca. Sharon Olds, Naomi Shihab Nye. I am in the audience again at a hundred readings, videos, podcasts, and talks.

Doesn't everyone have all of Shakespeare's plays, in a single volume complete works as well as the individual plays? How do you live without bookshelves lined with verse and reference books . . . just in case you need to dig out an evasive memory or *mot juste*? I roll the titles over on my tongue with new savor, a bit of nostalgia, and longing. It's like *déjà lu* all over again.

Summer Is a Raft

EVERY SO OFTEN, IT'S GOOD to let yourself drift, to just follow the current and see where it takes you; to leave an hour, a morning, a day unplanned; to enter open space and time and invite its effects. The artist Paul Klee spoke of drawing as "taking a line out for a walk." We can see his art as exploration, inquiry, following a random thought, or drifting—and look what comes of it: something fresh and new. This is what summer is for.

It's not always easy to do. I used to call time and space "boredom" when I was a kid, as in "Mom, I'm bored. There's nothing to do." Now I long for the chance to say, "There's nothing to do (i.e. nothing I *must* do) . . . thank goodness." Boredom has gotten such a bad rap. Kids are so conditioned to think that they must always be doing something, going somewhere, entertained, and active. But a little boredom can be a terrific vessel for a good drift, following a line of thoughts and just seeing what pictures appear.

It helps to have a raft in your summer—literally or figuratively. There were countless days when my boyhood gang, bored with the possibilities at home, gathered around Hurley's pond to throw planks together for epic raft voyages along its great gray-green greasy banks. Kids of a certain age have an instinctual urge to mess around on things that float, with mud, and with sticks.

Combine the three and you have an empire of imaginary possibilities. We could be Ulysses, Captain Hook, or Viking swashbucklers. Who needs PlayStation when you have a raft and a stick.

Later, when I read about Huck Finn, I learned that a raft is a moment on the Big River when the bravest adventure occurs: a true connection with another human being. For instance, Jim comes alive to Huck as a person, not just a slave, when they share the raft. A raft can be a collection of planks on the Mississippi, a moment of inspiration, or a yielding to a current that brings you around the bend to a new view of a person, place, or thing; a new settlement. One shouldn't gloss over the perils and cruelties encountered on Huck's trip down river. But we can safely say that it's good to have had a raft, to have drifted, been a swashbuckler, made brave connections.

From a vantage point of the prime meridian of summer, I like to listen to Huck's own words. Dip your toes with me in the current and eddies of his syntax, as Huck throws us an idyllic line:

"You feel mighty free and easy and comfortable on a raft. . . . Two or three days and nights went by; I reckon I might say they swum by, they slid along so quiet and smooth and lovely. Here is the way we put in the time. It was a monstrous big river down there—sometimes a mile and a half wide; we run nights, and laid up and hid day-times; soon as night was most gone, we stopped navigating and tied up—nearly always in the dead water under a towhead; and then cut young cotton-woods and willows and hid the raft with them. Then we set out the lines. Next we slid into the river and had a swim, so as to freshen up and cool off; then we set down on the sandy bottom where the water was about knee deep, and watched the daylight come. Not a sound, anywheres—perfectly still—just like the whole world was asleep, only sometimes the bull-frogs a-cluttering, maybe."

May the bullfrogs a-clutter to you, as you tend your lines, swim, cool off, and listen to the sound of "not a sound, any-wheres." May you find this free and easy feeling, and a respite from navigating in summer.

Ode to
Disraeli Gears

THE BEATLES ON ED SULLIVAN; Jimi at Monterey; Live at Leeds (If you have to ask, I cannot tell you)—all sonic, performance breakthroughs, one might call them; lyric awakening; rock and roll invasions of my personal history. I might as well have been eating my madeleines and soaking them in my tea as I recall my first listen to *Disraeli Gears*[1] stirred by its appearance in my Facebook feed last week. The cover art alone elicited an ecstatic memory.

I was in the seventh grade when the second album by Cream burst into my listening realm, back in the era of cover artwork as cultural signifiers and even political statement. Social media had yet to be invented, but I suppose album art could be a precursor. There was so much to see, listen to, and incorporate into my life. "Sunshine of your love" was in heavy rotation on my FM radio station and the turntable in my bedroom. In the car, it meant "Dad! Turn it up!" The pink and orange collage of faces and wings radicalized the cover art for my next book report in Mr. Katz's language arts class. It qualifies as a seminal moment. Turn it up indeed.

Ginger Baker's libidinal, syncopated drumming had me at hello—his massive (for the time) Ludwig kit, his four stroke ruffs, laying off the cymbals in favor of thrumming tom-toms and circumferencial rolls around the drum set's "equator." I wanted to drum like him. I painted my bass drum head with similar dayglow colors and swirling shapes. I borrowed drums to assemble a Ginger-sized kit. I even had naturally ginger hair.

Jack Bruce had a voice too good for rock and roll. It soared and vibrated. His bass was a lead instrument. He and Ginger, more than a rhythm section, went on attack. Eric Clapton—AKA God, "The Governor" to his generation of British blues men—had a tonal distinction (Gibson guitars and wall of black Marshall amps) plus riffs that rewrote the blues for my generation. Imagine discovering the African American blues masters via skinny British blokes.

Cream's frequent lyricist, beat poet Pete Brown, died recently, summoning the fantastical lyrics of "Tales of Brave Ulysses," "Sunshine of Your Love," "White Room." He also penned "Theme for an Imaginary Western." Recorded by both Mountain and Jack Bruce, it's an epic heavy metal reference to British bands touring in vans as if they were heading across the great plains for the western frontier in covered wagons. Epic thematic mash-up. Go west, young man—with your band.

Wheels of Fire, Cream's 1968 double album, included a live concert at Fillmore East, joined the influencers in my record collection. The band dove deep into soloing and riffing back and forth, including Ginger's drum solo: *"Toad."* Didn't I pore over that album-side cut seeking rhythms and techniques!

Back in American suburban basements, we wannabe power trios spent hours trying to cop the licks of our guitar and drum heroes. The basic chord structure and rhythmic backbone were one thing, but when it came time for the solo we rarely had their chops. Or the wah-wah pedal, which I don't recall hearing prior to DG. Each song's obligatory guitar solo back then had a narrative arc. It was storytelling, not just fretboard pyrotechnics like today's shredding masters—all arpeggio, little arc of feeling. Eric's solos plied the soul of the matter, usually love.

Why is this an ode? James Parker puts it precisely. We all have odes to explore and express. "They're swimming in your ambience," he writes in *The Atlantic*. "They want to be written, but only by you. There's an everlasting valentine at the nucleus of creation, and it's got your name on it." Odes bind the sum of your parts.

Parker continues his "ode to odes: "The point is, ode writing is a two-way street. The universe will disclose itself to you, it will give you occasions for odes, it will blaze with interest and appreciability, but you've got to be ode-ready. You've got to bring some twang, some perceptual innocence, some not-worn-out words. Respond to the essence with your essence, with the immaculate awareness that is your birthright. And on the days when the immaculate awareness is crap-encrusted, write an ode about that."

So many nucleic musical valentines, so little time. An ode is a form of gratitude. The rock and roll album/band/drummer odes alone require pages and pages giving thanks for the sonic breakthroughs in my life. You?

NOTE

1. The name comes from a Cream roadie misunderstanding Eric Clapton's reference to derailleur gears on his new racing bicycle.

As Poetry Is
My Compass

I WAS AT OUTWARD BOUND IN SCOTLAND, age 14, when I learned to use an orienteering compass. It mattered, hiking in the Cairngorm mountains and Western Highlands. Precise understanding of where you are and where you were intending to go, and location of the dangers that might prevent the meeting of the twain—cliffs, peat bogs, ravines laying in misty ambush—was crucial.

I remember the mnemonic taught for switching from the magnetic readings of the compass to the Ordinance Survey maps we used for navigating: "Mag to grid, get rid; grid to mag, add." That is, alter the reading by the number of degrees difference between North on the map, grid, and magnetic North of the compass. A minor calculation, but it could be the difference between walking over a ledge into thin air and finding a suitable course through the heather and bracken. It remains my emblem for all directional guidance.

I'm still a map guy, and I like using the cardinal directions: "We're a few miles south of that . . . go North two miles, then East." Or, "take the first turn northbound off the old county road." Maps carry legends. Forget your GPS and satellite-infused smartphone maps. Which side of the tree does the moss grow on anyway? Suppose your phone battery dies? Magnetic north pierces the mists.

I've supplied my kids with orienteering compasses, and the recommendation, "Don't leave home without it." Put it in your pocket along with your jackknife, my other standard equipment and graduation present. You're welcome. If you know where you are, you can plot a course to where you'd like to go. If you can see where you'd like to go, you can plot a course from where you are. It's a good metaphor too.

Poetry is a compass—internal, portable; part of the intergenerational script we've been installing for eons. Is there a compass of the heart? Of course—The bards have it. And troubadours, like those in the civil rights era I grew up in. "If I had a hammer," or "We shall overcome," to say nothing of the true north of the blues. One need not even add "moral" to "compass." To what would an immoral compass point?

Often a pithy maxim can also become a directional standard. My kids will cite two, ringing in their ears. "What is the point of highest leverage?" and "Fiscal sobriety." The first is the choice from which all downstream experiences flow—the new course and best chance at getting home safely. It counsels awareness of the moment and the fork in the road—orienteering, again. The latter is, no doubt, an inheritance of our Scottish thrift gene.

We were the people who left, at least in our surficial journeys. In some branches of our family tree, charted back 14 generations, "our" compass pointed to safety and opportunity—mag to grid. We left slums and oppression in numerous old countries; or jumped on a ship or covered wagon heading for the widening gyre of historical, religious, or economic opportunity. My generation owes its benefits to the compass of ancestors at points of highest leverage, though they may not have seen it that way. And we wish the best for our heirs.

When I share collected poems every Christmas they are like Ordinance Survey maps of the heart for my children. My favorite compass poem is "The Silken Tent," Robert Frost's single-sentence sonnet uniting the invisible magnetic attraction above us all in "She," the poem's central subject. It melds the figures of tent, woman, and text, rigid yet flowing, in a gentle doting—the poem itself becoming the compass, guiding us to the soul of its meaning,

> *By countless silken ties of love and thought*
> *To everyone on earth the compass round,*
> *And only by one's going slightly taut*
> *In the capriciousness of summer air*
> *Is of the slightest bondage made aware.*

Such orienteering. Its 14 lines have been my point of highest leverage many a time, and a kind of capital surplus, love being the ultimate wealth—not unlike a poem in which form and function, sound and sense unite effortlessly as a gentle course through the heather—a flawless mnemonic for surficial map and invisible coordinates. The poem maps my heart.

The Mighty Pen

WHEN I SIGN MY NAME—on a note, a letter, a legal document—I insist on using a certain pen. Signing tends to be the most handwriting I do, these days, since my laptop is faster and far neater for extensive written expression. I'm a fast typist. But a signature is different—my mark—and my pen is my emblem of writing, and more.

"Pen" means fountain pen. I have a small collection, purchased on special trips to remind me of a day and time in a unique place: Milan (the green Delta pen), Paris's Left Bank (the small yellow Jean Pierre Lépine pen), Glasgow (the transparent Pelikan). I can picture the shop, the street, the ambience of the day each pen joined my life.

Not all signing is alike, nor all signing pens. We sign letters and notes; sometimes documents with weightier intent: the mortgage, the employment contract, the marriage license—documents of exalted ilk. These require a *signing* pen. In my case, they require my father's Mont Blanc Meisterstück, the plump, black, gold filigreed, classic fountain pen with the iconic white star on the end of the cap.

I had not known he owned one, until after his passing. And the more I think about it, the more significance it adds to his life, and now to mine. A Mont Blanc pen is the apotheosis of "fountain pen." For me, like his Royal typewriter, another family emblem, it is the imprimatur of Dad.

That he owned such a luxurious pen, with his initials engraved on the gold clip, was news. He was thrifty, never spending more than required on a pair of shoes, a tool, or piece of equipment, sometimes to my chagrin. But his fountain pen was different. At some point he had splurged. Was it a token of accomplishment, a reward, something that spoke to his primal talent and passion, writing? And not just writing but *hand*writing.

Dad was a journalist—print, radio, television. And he had the most distinctive handwriting I've ever seen, recognizable instantly when I still find it in his marginalia, or signatures on old letters. He spoke Russian and had a handwriting style in English reminiscent of the Cyrillic alphabet. His signature had a rhythmic, circulating flourish that bespoke pleasure in the act of making letters and words.

My sister found the pen among his belongings. It reminded me of how special it was to sit at Dad's desk when I was a kid, rummaging in the drawers among his calligraphy pens and their myriad interchangeable points, and bottles of India ink that seemed from an archaic era of penmanship. He loved creating ornate letters, and once took a course in Chinese calligraphy. When I got married, he wrote a Chinese proverb with a calligraphy brush, on a long banner, for Lesley and me: "May you get white hair together." We have. Writing made it so.

Owl Time

MINERVA WAS BACK. And by the time I noticed her, perched in a decrepit spruce tree adjacent to my bird feeder, she may have been back for quite a while. And she lingered, perched long enough for me to pull up a chair by the window and observe her for quite a while.

Or, is it I who am back? For all I know she has been there all winter and I am the one who has been away, in her estimation—with the windows shut and owl sounds blocked or remote since last fall. As we open the windows of summer, we rejoin the avian audience.

Even the deer traipsing across the yard did not distract her from . . . what? Watching, like the Lionel Messi of birds, apparently doing nothing and preoccupied with things far from the game—but that's his winning technique. And just when you think an owl is asleep, she'll whip her head around in the direction of some imperceptible woodland chirp or scurry to make a scoring play. The mice have little defense but silence and stillness and hopeful thinking. They'll never know what ate them. An owl has serrated feathers that make their flight inaudible. But they might hear the famous question: "Who cooks for you?" echoing from above. No one cooks. Dinner is mouse carpaccio.

"My" owl always seems to be sitting on a branch where least expected.

One day, that happened to be on a level branch in the oak at the end of my yard—a superb hunting blind. The bark is gripped and scuffed from use. For another rendezvous, it's high up in my apple tree, a foggy blur on gnarly limbs. But every perch must have a direct line of sight on the ground where the chipmunks, mice, voles, and red squirrels feed. An owl manages to simultaneously be part of the foreground and background of the view, or secreted in a corner of the scene, like the horse in Breughel.

One has the feeling that by the time you realize you are, in fact, watching an owl, the owl has already been watching you for quite a while. Try and sneak up on an owl. They know your plan before you do. You cannot out-clandestine an owl.

Was this the same owl who made a ghostly appearance on my trail camera over the winter, wings extended in a midnight swoop on a hapless critter? Hard to tell. She was caught in a flash with that same inscrutable gaze—then flew off.

Several Barred owls were calling last night from deeper in the woods, that special evening tide alert to fellow owls across the field and hiding in the opposite spruces. Time to be up and hunting. I look forward to my summer owl patrol, sitting in my dooryard listening and watching, hoping for a glimpse, but it's great just to have their sounds infiltrating my space.

It's a full-time job waiting for an owl to appear or reappear; listening for the dusk serenade; pretending to be having a conversation, however one-sided.

Writer's Block

I MUST WRITE SOMETHING TODAY.

Some days commence with that feeling, as if words are waiting—noisy and persistent—in the wings, eager to make an appearance, to be woven into sentences and paragraphs. They are wearing their costumes—What feathers! Sequins, even!—and mouthing their lines while peering past the curtains stage left for a peek at the audience.

No matter that the sun is out for the first time since March; that the oak trees finally have their leaves; that the brook trout will finally be feeding at the surface of McCaslin Brook above the beaver dam, as mayflies hatch; that breezes on the harbor augur good sailing—or just pleasant foraging for pottery shards, shells, rocks, and driftwood on the backshore beach.

Surely it's a better day for a picnic in the field under Arthur Wardwell's oak tree by Hatch Cove, or for playing hooky from words and climbing Blue Hill where the lupine are exploding into bloom and the islands of Penobscot Bay will look like floating porcupines moored in the lustrous, blueberry-dark sea.

Never mind that the vegetable garden needs planting, or that our new raspberry plants have been languishing in their pots from the nursery while patiently waiting for just such a day as this to be snuggled into soil. Already sending out new suckers, the plants have blossomed and are swelling with emerging berries. In a month, they could be ready for picking! Yes, today would be a great day to start our very own berry patch.

Or a pumpkin patch. Last year's pumpkins in our new garden were pitiful and stunted, but, with the "spring dressing," cover crop, and organic matter carefully folded into the field this month, we hope to be raising some true jack-o-lanterns by Halloween. Perhaps some of Fred Cole's magic seeds from his blue ribbon pumpkins at the fair—they were the size of an Airstream trailer—would flourish this summer, if we planted now.

Yes, it's a summer day, finally. Such days work a charm on my friend Sam, who lives in Manhattan, and would say: "This is a good day to cross water and walk on grass." By which bridge? Brooklyn, George Washington, Williamsburg, Tri-borough, Queensboro? How about Deer Isle.

The bridge to Deer Isle stretches like an inverted hammock across Eggemoggin Reach. It leads to the granite ledges around Sunshine—good swimming in August—and Eaton's lobster pound, or the harbor in Stonington. This would be a good day to sketch the lobster boats at the dock, or the fishermen's cottages on Water Street.

But that'll have to be a road not taken—there are words insistently waiting for their chance to be heard.

Is "hammocking" a word? It should be. *Hammocking* between two of our hackmatack trees is the best spot from which to *binocular* birds. Binocular should be a verb. Hammocked in stillness, I never fail to spot unusual, stealthy birds flitting across the pine canopy. Last week, an over-flight of three great blue herons was my reward for languorous patience, and a marsh hawk perched atop a broken fir tree planning his next hunting sortie. It has been a good bird week, starting with the three osprey I spotted fishing near Flye Point yesterday morning. Later, a bald eagle sailed up the field by my office, at roof level, his shadow no doubt terrorizing the rabbits and mice foraging in the meadow grass below.

Poems must arrive on similar wings, casting their sharp eye on the field of paper, pondering whether to swoop to earth on extended wings or alight on a brittle branch. Perhaps it was a day like this when Ted Hughes was visited by "The Thought Fox," which came "about its own business," and left the poet's page mysteriously, delicately printed. Or perhaps a poem arrives as a fish peering through its glassy ceiling, wondering at a world of all air, even while swaying in midcurrent—and feeding, eating even as it avoids being eaten by another . . . thought.

Words must have been waiting in the wings to talk about themselves in Elinor Wylie's imagination when she said "I love smooth words, like gold-enameled fish/Which circle slowly with a silken swish."

Just so, words are waiting in the wings, circling slowly in my thoughts. *I feel I really must write something today, if only to mention that certain slant of dawn light by the back porch humming-bird feeder, or last night's firefly quasars hovering over the clover outside this window.*

The Return of Background Sounds

"THE BEST PART OF GOING OUT TO EAT ONCE MORE," said my friend David, "was just being among fellow diners." He was describing the fellowship rediscovered in his first post-pandemic return to a restaurant. Of particular pleasure: the familiar ambient sounds that had been missing from life during the year "the locust had eaten." How we forget the granularity, the texture of being *among* other people. How good it feels to be reunited. We've been away, dining alone, tired of our own company.

Consider the restaurant sounds you've missed—the hubbub of tabled conversation; the clatter of dishes and cutlery, taking of orders, clink of glasses; ice cubes. The aromas! What's cooking? Breaking bread together is restorative—a reunion with the companionship of being among others, dispensing with the artificial congregations of remote, virtual, or distanced gatherings. We are rubbing elbows, occupying the same space, restoring the customary background noises and close encounters of the dining out kind. It's touching.

An online wine tasting just appeared in my e-news feed. Nope. The invitation to a virtual college reunion leaves me cold. Oh, to hear "Do you have a reservation?" "Your table is ready." "Would you like to hear our specials tonight?" Table for one in the wilderness—over.

To think, *What that couple are having certainly looks good. Yes, I'll have what they're having . . . rather than the leftover leftovers chez moi.* It made me think of other public-place, congregant sounds. I took a mental inventory of what I had been missing; what we are about to be reacquainted with.

For one thing, it's a good year to celebrate *Le Quatorze Juillet* and liberation from the Covid-Bastille. "Allons enfants de la patrie, Le jour de gloire est arrivé!" Vive normalité.

Another: The crack of the bat and, as the ball arcs over the stretching second baseman's glove, the rising roar of the crowd—a base hit . . . a double! The crowd's clapping, cheers, crescendos, then the sonic wave settles back as the ballpark organist takes up the ascending chords of the chant and the next batter digs in for his ups, and maybe an RBI—and it's not the canned crowd noises from an archived game, like the laugh track instead of a live studio audience. It's *this* game. Now. Here. We are among one another, again, not the crowd of cut-outs sitting in the stands. It's the real thing responding to *this* game. Time out is over. Take me out to the *crowd*. Play ball.

Or consider our estrangement from exploring a new street, overhearing conversations by strangers, in a language you don't speak; the unfamiliar sounds of foreign taxis and buses and sirens, the fragrance of exhaust and bakeries mingling. Even a pipe, cigar, or cigarette gives an olfactory frisson, a guilty whiff of other people's health transgressions. In our isolation, there was no second-hand smoke, overheard conversation, or spontaneous witnessing of emotion. It's all been piped in, packaged, filtered, pre-determined—no more. We are done with filtered experience.

Even the murmuration of readers in a used book store or library loitering in the stacks, thumbing pages, and pulling a surprise title off the shelf. It's the feeling of group browsing. It might be the ambient non-sound of perusing together in a place we expect to be a little dark, a little musty, and comfortable. But it's witnessing *sharing*. Oh, to sit among the quiet readers in the comfy chairs of the periodical section. Who knew it would be a *thing*. Perhaps there is a barista steaming milk or grinding the espresso . . . even the vibe of a background playlist and the chit chat at café tables welcomes.

And then there are congregations themselves: Church. Hang up the virtual choir and let harmony ring in true choral singing. Simply sitting in the pews, *en masse,* is restorative. Responsive reading, and its fellowship, is communion with ourselves. Words of hymns are beneficial, but there is a gestalt to singing together. It goes beyond . . . the timbre of voices and the swell of the accompaniment. In Excelsis exhalation Deo.

The ambient background sounds we miss are not our tired solo sounds; not the household ticks and tocks (does anyone still have a clock that ticks?) of isolation. The forlorn fridge hums; the dog's tail beats the floor; the fire crackles in the grate. This ambience of solitude that used to sound so comforting when life was overstimulating and hectic, is not. We are no longer scrolling a feed of remote updates, we are back to people watching, and people hearing. No more, "I hear you, but I can't see you. . . ." Or, "Connection is Unstable." We've had enough of the virtual version of the world, at long last, for now—"zoom fatigue" we embrace you. Let us now mingle and pour out. Congregation is back better—to stay, one hopes.

Taking a Walk
with Clark
Fitz-Gerald

ONE THING JUST LED TO ANOTHER after Liddy Fitz-Gerald
visited school on Monday with a box of her husband Clark's
miniature sculptures. Clark's full-sized works can be found in
public spaces ranging from Philadelphia to Coventry Cathedral.
Now the table in my office had become a mini gallery of the 32
small objects that inspired huge public art.

At some point, Liddy had made up a word for them: jibbies.
Here were nature's forms and functions isolated on a small
wooden pedestal.

Here was the stone with pebble-worn tunnels, the fossil clam-
shell, the sea purse; the scroll of a leaf, its veins curled inward like
a hand. Another leaf suggests the prow of a Viking long boat. A
chip of wood, a piece of bark, a geester in mid seed-dispersal, a
dried starfish, petrified worm castings—they had all interrupted
a walk with Clark, who would pocket them for his collection
and then reimagine them as monuments or soaring carvings.
Even spirals of brass, snipped from some routine sheet that Clark

was turning into an exotic form, were exalted when they became minute Mobius strips.

Of course, there are plenty of human forms walking around Castine, Maine. They are flesh and blood jibbies, I suppose, that have turned up in Clark's curvaceous carvings of elm trees. The town crew used to drop off massive tree trunks at his studio, salvaged from the dump for art's sake.

The kids at my school started to come by for a look. When second grader Dustin saw them he said, "You can make art out of anything." True, if you have the right eyes. A walk with Clark, it turns out, wasn't about getting anywhere in particular—it was about *seeing* things. Really seeing things. Botany or paleontology or geology might be the formal name for such science, but it's actually a matter of art, or poetry, or music—seeing, or feeling, or hearing a different pulse in things.

So, I opened the Clark Fitz-Gerald Table Top Gallery in my office. When Tom, a parent in my school, saw it, he immediately appreciated the "childlike wonder" evident in Clark's choice of natural objects. The kindergartners came two by two and looked at the little forms, and the shadows they were making on the table. With awe, they recognized familiar objects from their own beach combing.

Where might this lead? I cut some wooden pedestals and started to hand them out as other classes came for a gallery visit. Mrs. Belyea's art classes picked up the work, gleaning along the town common and adjacent neighborhood for significant *objets d'art*. Within hours we had produced our own original jibbies: pebbles, maple leaves, horse chestnut hulls, twigs, black locust seed pods, lichens . . . even a few bottle caps. Sculpture was to be found everywhere.

By Friday, Mrs. Pelletier's second and third graders were ready for a walk to the maritime academy across town in search of full-scale works by Clark. It wasn't hard to spot the curve of the mussel shell in the two-story welded weather station sculpture, or the spiny sea urchin in the ornate grill above the library entrance. And in the lobby of one building, we recognized the whale vertebrae abstracted by Clark as an almost human form. The kids pulled out their clipboards and got to work sketching. One good sculptural line deserved another at the end of a third grader's pencil.

The appreciation and insight in our strolls with Clark reminded me of a sentence by Lewis Thomas, who could intertwine unheard melodies and things from the natural world in his musings. "If we had better hearing," he wrote, "and could discern the descants of sea birds, the rhythmic timpani of schools of mollusks, or even the distant harmonics of midges hanging over meadows in the sun, the combined sound might lift us off our feet."

Though he's been gone for many years now, I like to think Clark is still making extraordinary art in a new studio. We can imagine the new jibbies he'll certainly be finding, arranged in the morning light filtering into a new studio, and the grand sculptures that will be coaxed from some new leaf, or mollusk, or stone. The school kids can carry on the local work. "Lifted" is the right word for our experience. In December, we put our jibbies on display alongside Clark's at the public library. A simple stroll on the common or down Court Street has yielded a new generation of jibbies: Chestnut husks elevated to medieval armor, an elm leaf as imperial emblem, a scrap of bark as winter ocean wave. Childlike wonder lives, as we all take a walk with Clark, like Clark. Do you hear timpani too?

Speak, Matryoshka Memory

FOR ME, IT BEGINS WITH A MAP. In third grade, I had a large wall map of Russia next to my bed. My reading light shone over Ukraine, Siberia, the border republics to the south. And I recall lying in bed perusing the exotic place names, rivers, lakes, mountain ranges, and sprawling landmass and borders of The Union of Soviet Socialist Republics. It was detailed, beautifully drawn, and an emblem of my dad's fascination with Russian history and language. Scanning it on my way to sleep, I could hear Dad in his study working on his textbook: *The USSR and Communism.* It was the early 1960s.

I remember his distinctions between contemporary *Soviet* Russia, and the Russia of the steppes, the Tsars, the harsh climates, Tolstoy and Dostoyevsky and Tchiakovsky. Russia has 11 time zones. The vast Trans-Siberian Railroad. Vladivostok was fun to say. "The Russians Are Coming, The Russians Are Coming" was the favorite movie in our house, growing up, and we played a lot of records by Russian folk singer Theodore

Bikel, who I met once in Chicago. I brought along my bongos to play for him.

Dad studied Russian as a high school student in Buffalo, and then, as the post-World War II world took shape in the 1950s, prepared himself in college and graduate school for what would be The Big International Political Story for an aspiring journalist: Soviet-U.S. relations. Nothing in our family background predicts this interest. We are not Russian.

By the spring of 1972, Dad was a foreign correspondent in London. Living closer to the USSR, he planned to take my brother and me on a package tour: Sochi, on the Black Sea, Moscow, and Leningrad. Alas, it was not to be. The Soviet embassy denied his visa request, probably because Brezhnev and Nixon were meeting in Moscow as part of their détente initiative. No more journalists need apply—a sub-plot of Soviet-American relations.

Russia came into focus again in the 1980s when Dad was hired by the Kettering Foundation to write the history of its "six decades . . . providing private citizens of Russia and the United States a forum for sustained, substantive discussion and debate on issues critical to their nations and to world peace." He finally got to visit Russia.

He left an annotated photographic record of his visits. For me, the visual high point is his photo standing beside Yevgeny Yevtushenko at the poet's dacha, the poet holding an apple core, eating while expounding. The casual tourist snapshots include St. Basil's, the Kremlin, Lenin's tomb, Gum department store, the winter palace in Leningrad, and street scenes of daily life.

Dad meticulously labeled each photo: "Blagovyeshtchenski Cathedral. Tsars were christened and married here. Founded 1397. Rebuilt 1482–89. The Gold is Real." Ever the reporter, in his caption I hear his voice emphasizing the length of Russian memory and history. In another caption, he seemed to invoke the journalistic voice-over he might have used for a panoramic video shot: "The scene is Red Square, Moscow, the view toward St. Basil's Russian Orthodox cathedral, upstaged by ranks of Intourist buses." It had setting, historical scene, and ironic commentary. Here's another: "The rear of the Winter Palace, now the Hermitage art museum. Where the workers overthrew the Provisional Government in 1917." You are there, with Dad.

By the 1990s, my teaching career had taken us to Chicago. On cab rides to O'Hare airport I often found myself in conversation with drivers who might be, say, former Russian computer programmers. "My dad speaks Russian," I delighted in sharing. Dad enjoyed conversing with them too—in Russian. On one visit, he met Ludmila, an émigré who worked with my wife. Dad delighted in conversation over dinner, discussing the nuances of Russian vowel sounds and pronunciation. "Onion" must have been on the menu, and a linguistic case in point.

This is the other Russia-Dad story: the sheer pleasure of conversation, inter-personal connection, breaking bread, and sharing a table—with a language, with a history, with a people, and finally with oneself.

I rediscovered the old cherished map rolled up in a tube, suitable for framing in an essay. Its borders are obsolete; Soviet era republic names changed; but it's still suitable for a few moments touring the Union of Russo-Nelson Experiences. I've peeled an onion of recollection. Speak, Matryoshka doll of memory, Nabokov might say. But am I the singular little doll at the heart, or the big doll containing all the others? Each, and all. Ride the Trans Nelson-Russia railway to Vladivostok—from Buffalo, to Chicago, to Boston, Dayton, London, and Moscow. It terminates in Vladivostok—still fun to say, and far, far away. That sounds like a caption "our hero" might write.

The Augurs of Green Man Day

I RECALL IT WITH CLARITY AND JOY—the sunny day in May, 1968 that altered my life. My personal history is divided between Before and After Green Man Day—my crossing of the Rubicon of ecstatic, improvisational play—the day when Jimmy Butler and I painted our faces green at the seventh grade arts festival. It was also the year of *The White Album* and *Electric Ladyland*, for those of you who mark the passing of time with musical correlatives. I do. Whose albums? If you have to ask, you can't be told.

What *were* we thinking? What could possibly have inspired us?

First, it was an astoundingly vibrant and unusual day of school. All the regular classes were supplanted with special arts activities. We weren't even using the usual Junior High School facility, but an alternative location. It was a workshop day. We were *making* things, painting things, constructing and collaging and weaving things; *doing* things with our hands. It was a day when there was a skill and behavior inversion: the kids who sat at the back of the room and were quiet, those who learned better with their hands, became more vocal and active and vital. The kids who always had their hands in the air with the right answer to the teacher-posed questions were off balance.

Suddenly, *all* the multiple intelligences, instead of just the customary book-learnin' ones, were in bold relief. And this was about 20 years before anyone was even talking about different *kinds* of intelligence. I can only imagine the rancorous faculty meetings involved in creating this event.

And there we were, Jimmy Butler and me standing at the paint table wondering what to do with our intelligent hands. We began sounding our "barbaric yawp." We entered the Amazon rainforest of our improvisational desires and came out painted like tribal warrior princes. It must have followed some kind of, "I will if you will," or even the Double Dog Dare. We both would; we both did. We both dared to go green.

It signified independence and autonomy, and certainly a loss of inhibition. It was about the intangibles of youth . . . the moments when we discover our own voice, make a choice, select a character to play, a costume, if only briefly. It was tentative risk taking; it was forging identity separate from peers and parents. Perhaps it was the onset of my recognition that academic curricula come and go; the broader work of greening identity and establishing a sense of individual possibility for our lives is the true long-term study.

It's also simply great, sticky, gooey, glorious fun: paint smells good, feels good, and attracts attention when it appears in unexpected places. And the females of our species took notice of our exotic plumage.

Soon I would be a drummer in a power-trio garage band. Rock and roll took the place of green face—but it was the same idea, viz Kiss, Bowie, and bands of that nascent ilk. The green paint washed off, after a very effective surprise for Mom when I got off the school bus. But clearly, the new tint of personal legend has lingered. And, as I recall, it led shortly thereafter to a purple shirt and chartreuse bellbottoms worn with pride to the first day of eighth grade. Green Man Day was a delightfully slippery slope.

The Heist: Organized Crime in Penobscot

I'D LIKE TO REPORT A ROBBERY. Grand theft. Conspiracy even!
The crows were the tip-off. When they show up on the ground
beneath my bird feeder, I know the squirrels have come and gone,
spraying my premium black oil sunflower seeds in a 360-degree
arc for all to pilfer. They crack the "warehouse" and get the heist
under way. The law-abiding chickadees still come and go in an
orderly fashion, up and down their glide paths from the maples
and firs—polite, appreciative, and taking only what they can fly
with. The brazen squirrels, however, are clearly hoarding, judging by their rotund bellies and paunch. I begrudge them.

I know a squirrel-crow crime syndicate when I see one. And
perhaps more. Red squirrels are not guiltless; chipmunks and
mice have tunneled beneath the snow to access the bounty from
below. Their access routes radiate out like metropolitan com-
muter routes around Boston. Soon a fox learns of their where-
abouts and drops by for lunch. Now it's a deadly racket. An
owl follows, perched right on my back porch coldly eyeing the

tunnels. Apex predators were now in on the subsidiary benefits of the heist.

Who knows what raccoons, the usual suspects, might be doing in their unwitnessed midnight ramblings. Have I left anyone out? Seems like a victimless crime—but I know a perp walk when I see one. The squirrels are just asking for someone to drop a dime on them. Who you gonna call?

The mastermind and prime mover of this crime spree is obvious. Whether the crows are opportunistic or managerial is hard to discern; whether the squirrels enjoy some kick-back for their hack of my squirrel suppression scheme—a trash can lid hung above the feeder that hangs from a very thin wire—or are simply rogue actors abusing my benevolence. But they're in cahoots with the whole non-avian forest.

And Blue Jays too—another crime family appeared this week. The word is out. They swooped in for a hit-and-run raid on the sunflower seed grounds. They don't do anything without attracting attention to themselves and encouraging the squirrels. No subtlety in the blue jay crew. Don't even get me started on the wild turkey horde.

The deer always play innocent, as if they're just stumbling upon a free lunch and have no hand in the robbery planning or execution. Sometimes I see them at night, ghostly shapes joining the larceny. But I think they've been tipped off. Probably the squirrels again.

What's the "vig" for the criminal efforts of the portly rodents? They must get something in return. Surely they're not risking the ramping up of hostilities and annihilation for nothing. They wouldn't hijack a semi just for bragging rights—and my 40 pounds of seed is quite a haul. Consider all the acorn-gathering they *didn't* have to do this season, thanks to my unwilling largesse. I know racketeering when I see it.

I've gotten wind of an even bigger heist in the works. It's the Brinks Robbery of bird feeder pillage. When Bruno (or Barbara?) awake from their winter slumbers feeling a bit peckish, feeders like mine are ripe for targeting. It's open season. The bear—the oligarch of sunflower seed pillaging—will not shake loose just a few pounds of seed. They take down the whole feeder system. Last April, I awoke to find Bruno reclining on the ground, my feeder between his paws, sucking out the tasty morsels without a care in the world. You're welcome. Other years, the feeder has been demolished and abandoned in the woods at the end of a long trail of seed. And yes, they do leave the "processed seed" in the woods—seed laundering?

I'll give it a few more weeks and then pull the plug on the whole crime spree. Before Bruno awakens from his slumbers, I'll remove the feeder and stow it for next year. As the apex benefactor, I've managed to seize a little joy from the process. After all, every so often a weary species from away will drop by, blown off course by an upper atmosphere disturbance, needing a little sustenance. This year it was a flock of Evening Grosbeaks draining the feeder and then moving on. Even the squirrels couldn't get a snack while they were feasting at my brasserie.

On the other hand, this might be interstate trafficking. Add that to wire fraud and murder Inc. And who says there's no free lunch? Wise guys. And the squirrel? I'll get him on tax evasion. Warrant in hand. Time for the perp walk.

In Just Seventh Grade

I AM IN SEVENTH GRADE LANGUAGE ARTS class, an upstairs room in the old red brick junior high school building. The afternoon sun streams through its high windows that face onto the playground and athletic fields. It is the day I remember hearing a phrase for the first time: "the little lame balloon man." It comes from "In Just," the poem we are reading in our anthology and Mr. Katz is trying to loosen up our adolescent imaginations to the point where we might appreciate figurative language. Why are "eddieandbill . . . running from marbles and piracies?" It's not, evidently, a spelling or grammar question.

Then along comes another phrase: "the world is mudlucious," then "puddle-wonderful," and "bettyandisbel come dancing from hop-scotch and jump-rope." And something begins to blossom in me as a reader: the melding of descriptive words and words embodying action. Words could be and do what they describe! The April day effortlessly bespoke the poem, and the poem bespoke the day. I'd like to think Mr. Katz was conspiring with the poem, sun, spring, and kid energy. Not just lesson plan. Whichever—so be it. From thenceforth, I was a new reader and writer. I look back on that poem as a starting line. I heard the call to poetry.

I will begin seeing "In Just" by e.e. cummings in practically every subsequent anthology in my language arts life in high school and college and teaching. It was in my dog-eared *Pocket Book of Modern Verse* edited by Oscar Williams (high school); in *An Approach to Poetry* by Wayne Shumaker (freshman year survey course, college); *An Introduction to Poetry* by X.J. Kennedy (teaching); and *The Language of Spring: Poems for the Season of Renewal* which I just acquired. And it is, of course, in the *Complete Poems of e.e. cummings*, a Christmas present my senior year in high school. It is not included in *The Oxford Book of American Literature*. Pity. They all reside on my shelves, a chronology of anthologies; a syllabus of my reading life.

I began to realize that a poet is describing the world, experience, or concepts in a way that antidotes dullness, commonness, and indifference; that stretches the possibilities of language; that sings and beckons. A poem is a discrete vessel of clarity and understanding. "Poetry is the one permissible way of saying one thing and meaning another," Robert Frost explained, which I saw applied in poem after poem. Alternate universes abound. Rather, poems of all eras live in a kind of simultaneity in their anthologized universes.

Reading poems became a daily practice. I collect them, anthologizing my own favorite expressions of life's joys and tribulations—the record of thoughts, feelings, experiences of the most capable commentators on how to sail any waters. I'm fond of Billy Collins's view: "The history of poetry is the only surviving history we have of human emotion. It is the history of the human heart. There is no other one. Without poetry, we would be deprived of the emotional companionship of our ancestors."

Furthermore, as bipeds we walk in iambs and the four chambers of our heart cannot help but give us the tempo of a 4/4 march. We are intrinsically called to poetry. Ultimately, we *are* the anthology.

From the intervening decades of my teaching career, my "anthology" burgeons with poems I have taught, or that have taught me; that I have shared, or had shared with me; that gave me the insight and love, truth and beauty, of which poetry is uniquely capable. My criteria: poems must immediately reward having been read; be instantaneously valuable or impressive; sound good, or feel good, or go swiftly into one's mental hip pocket. I link poems to distinct times and places, people or experiences; a laugh, a slant of light, an inspiring or mirthful thought; a heartbreak or infatuation. I have an almanac of readings that are like stations in the metro.

Modern Verse became my go-to source for inspiration about beauty, integrity, irony, love—the distillations of thought and expression on the essence of truth. These were the great words, the memorable lines of insight; verbal treasure; a hoard of optimum English usage. Whoa! Now that is hifalutin praise. But it's true to my recollection of the tone of my discoveries. The anthology had mysteries and inscrutable purpose; language I had to wrestle with or research. But I intuited deep inner meanings and verbal power would be the reward. Often it was a closing line or stanza that accomplished the memorializing. Sometimes it's the narrative journey of the whole poem leading from scene to scene, moment to moment, feeling to feeling. Or a single delicious image.

We all know William Butler Yeats's oft quoted "The Second Coming"—"The falcon cannot hear the falconer. . . . the best lack all conviction." Or, "the Lake Isle of Innisfree: "I will arise and go now . . . the bee-loud glade" e.e. cummings is probably more often anthologized for "In Just" a poem about spring and the "little lame balloon man," but I've been more influenced by "pity this busy monster manunkind not/progress is a comfortable disease." He exits with "listen—there's a helluva good universe next door: let's go." I loved the wry grin in his final line, the antidote for the grim prognosis laid out before, a playful response to the harsh human condition, and my kind of quantum theory.

I loved W.H. Auden's closing line of "The Unknown Citizen": "Had anything been wrong we would certainly have heard." Richard Eberhardt reduced "the fury of aerial bombardment" to the cynical, terse mechanics of distinguishing "the belt feed lever from the belt holding pawl." I can stand with Thomas Hardy, perhaps best known as a Masterpiece Theater novelist and less as a lyric poet, as he surveys a new century and the portents of a birdsong in "The darkling thrush," as he leans upon a "coppice gate" in the west country of England—"Hardy Country." I spent a high school summer there working in a small country restaurant.

From "The Thought Fox" by Ted Hughes, I learned how the parallax world of observation can step onto the page leaving footprints in the form of memory and imagination. Marianne Moore did the same in "Poetry." "I too dislike it," she began, recommending a poesy of "Imaginary gardens with real toads in them." I'll never resolve that—thank goodness. Poetry sometimes belies our rational efforts. It is not science. Archibald MacLeish helps: "A poem should not mean, but be."

Now, my collection of poems is an emotional companion to my own life, myriad volumes documenting that companionship one poem at a time. The special ones even lead back to an inaugural memory of a sunny classroom in junior high school when Mr. Katz carefully broached new territory—a moment that suspended my preoccupation with middle-school mundanity. The dance on Friday, my drum lesson on Wednesday afternoon, and even Caroline's beguiling ponytail yielded. I was smitten with a poem. The "goat footed balloon man," still "whistles far and wee," makes the world "mudlucious" again and again, making spring a poetic rite. And every time, I come running.

My Life in Bicycles

I'VE ALWAYS HAD A BIKE. Surely, I started with a tricycle, like everyone aspiring to a two-wheeler, but I don't remember mine. The first bike I do remember was Greensleeves, a Schwinn cruiser with balloon tires and big fenders. The name? I don't recall. We lived in Evanston, Illinois then, where I could pedal along block after block of concrete sidewalk and square corners; alleys; and a few hypotenuse paths across the playground at my school: Lincolnwood Elementary school. Greensleeves was liberator, once Dad took off the training wheels.

In third grade, we moved to suburban Boston and I don't remember my green bike coming with us. But I do remember our first Christmas in a new house and neighborhood, and the Raleigh three-speed waiting for me under the tree. Suburban midwestern avenues became country lanes, curvy and hilly, and riding felt like a much grander adventure. The elegant, thin frame and classic leather seat of my Raleigh—with a gear shifter—was a quantum leap in style, mechanics, and bicycling élan.

I craved more speeds. By sixth grade, I had lawn-mowing money. I needed $64.00 to buy the gold Raleigh ten-speed, with the ram horn racing handlebars, from Pete Jacobs Sporting Goods. Mr. Jacobs would hold it for me in the store basement while I saved up—the first time I recall an earning/saving goal, even though my mother probably just bought it and told Pete to keep it off the showroom floor. Soon it was mine. Now I rode across town to my lawn mowing gig. I rode everywhere. I loved its leather racing seat; the bronze and cream paint; the trademark crest; the taped handlebars and brakes. I had that bike for a long time—from sixth grade to college.

In ninth grade we moved to London. My Raleigh came with us. I rode it to school down the left side of Cromwell Road to Knightsbridge. And that first summer, with my best friend Alan Fallow, conducted an epic bike trip. We rode from London to Land's End and back—southern coast out, northern coast back through the west country of England: Dorset, Devon, Cornwall, Somerset, and through Oxford back to London.

Days one and two were wretched. My back tire inner tube blew out hourly, until I found the embedded tack. Eventually, we enjoyed routine forty-mile days, even a few hundred-mile days, hugging the small farm roads, alternating between camping and youth hostels, peddling narrow hedge-rimmed lanes blocked with an occasional cow herd and its debris field.

We camped on Sennen Cove at Land's End and watched the sun set as a magical culmination. Would Sennen Cove and Tintagel Castle look the same today? Cruising in victory home through North London felt like a final lap on the Champs Elysees. Alas, no champagne, but an imaginary *maillot jaune* for each of us as we coasted through Hyde Park with iron thighs and sunburned forearms. Where did that bike go?

Next bike: a black Univega with kiddie seat on the back and wide tires. Solid. Sure, it had plenty of gears, and now I had plenty of baggage. Funny—I never had a bike helmet until now, and one for the kid, Spencer, playing bongos on my backside. Probably a good thing, as I accidently dumped us both on the ground one day.

That bike moved to California with us, then Evanston, again. I enjoyed rides by Lake Michigan and bike paths through the famous suburbs of John Hughes movies. By that time, Spencer was the rider. One day he took it to the local pet store, parked it outside, and entered to look at exotic birds. When he came out, the bike was gone, along with my leather jacket, Kryptonite lock, and lock key. That was a long walk home for Spencer. The day lives in infamy.

I still have a bike. It's a big, heavy L.L. Bean cruiser with an enormous basket on the front, like the ones our English greengrocer used to make home deliveries. Greensleeves II. I'll take a spin down the road every so often, but for the most part I use it as a time-saver to zip to the mailbox. The basket absorbs any packages and periodicals. It's useful, comfortable, and has a child seat on the back for a new generation riding behind, getting a feel for balance, peddling, and braking.

My favorite bike of all time, however, is the classic little red Peugeot stored in our basement. Its chrome fenders are rusted and tires flat as it awaits a new rider with training wheels and coaster brakes. It taught each of our kids to ride. Grampa Lowell bought it for Spencer, long ago. It reminds me of the two-wheeler in *Curious George Rides a Bike*. It won't take much to put it back on the road. Fresh inner tubes, a little chrome polish, some WD-40 on the chain, and we'll get the next generation into the peloton.

Snail Mail

Dear Reader:

There is nothing quite like *receiving* a letter; or *sending* a letter—a true letter, with envelope, and a postage stamp. Snail mail. That is, messing around with words, and the expectation one creates or experiences, for others and oneself. Letters have personality, texture, individuality, aroma, and require opening. Anticipation is part of the pleasure, and its back and forth, reciprocity, taking turns listening and talking. Letters may be the vinyl to email's digital recording, each one unique in ambience and presence, especially when handwritten.

In a home where typing was the dominant sonic background, letter writing was the family business. And I've always had a couple of ongoing postal correspondents, even in the age of email, which has flattened the world for me. It began in high school. We lived abroad for two years. The only way to keep in touch with my friends back in the states, or with my London friends who departed to the States, was Her Majesty's airmail.

I filed regular reports on my encounter with a new culture: currency, food, concerts, and a familiar language spoken with unfamiliar accents. Kathy moved to Australia and wrote long letters, Canberra to London, then Canberra to Boston. She wrote about school, transitions, the new country, and Led Zeppelin's tour of Australia complete with review of Bonzo's drum solo. Allan moved home to Maryland. We corresponded about school, transitions, familiar suburban lives, and Canned Heat concerts. I used to know my friends by their handwriting.

The supreme correspondence in my life lasted a year. I was in Scotland. Lesley Brody, my intended, was not. I think we single-handedly supported both the U.S.P.S. and the Royal Mail with our torrid, daily letters. The problem is, the seven-day delivery gap makes it impossible to be in synch. One's questions and answers are always past relevance by the time received. Best to stick to travel writing—describing events, activities, and inner monologues. Letter writing becomes journaling, an archival recording. And for a while, after a few years of marriage, ours were indeed archived. Classified. Then one night we decided they were extra baggage. Into the wood stove they went in a ritual burn, their purpose served, now too hot for posterity.

Today, I have letter-writing friends (some still use stationery!) and email-friends. And a special hybrid: the letter-writing emailers who eschew the brevity and haste of email conventions and compose complete sentences, and conventions of capitalization and punctuation gone by custom's wayside. Will there ever be a genre called "The Collected emails of . . . ?" I think not. Though, apparently, an email exists forever in the digital ether archive. Why bother?

Now, the U.S. Postal Service enhances anticipation with its daily email announcing what *will* be in the mailbox. The best of both worlds: electronic alerts for paper handling, and real envelopes worth trudging to the box at the end of the driveway to retrieve, on a good day. It's the Slow Word movement to correspond to Slow Food.

I gauge the era of former students by the mail they send—postcards and letters, or letter-like emails, from my earliest classes. Like me, they are not native to digital technology, but great with paper and pens. They know where to position the inside address on stationery. More recent students don't know the conventions of addressing an envelope—the levels of generality in a postal address. *It's just an outline!* What's an outline?

And so I was glad to see a properly addressed envelope and delightful letter from a recent graduate in today's mail. Correspondence lives, Huzzah! Sending a letter to your old English teacher is a fraught, Homeric labor. I know: I've done it. Mr. Walker was kind and appreciative of the outreach, with all my prior teaching and learning and proofreading on display. No pressure. He penned a response.

My friend Jeff, a London-era correspondent, now a "Michigander," is both an electronic and old-school letter writer. We both know what is stamp-worthy, versus what requires the immediacy and brevity of digital mail. He annotated a recent clipping (who even uses *that* word any more, for writing!): "I want to support the USPS." Long may the acronym wave—and the Harvard comma, proper capitalization, complex sentences; gerundive distancing, and *The Elements of Style*. Death to emojis. I may never, however, overcome the urge to correct grammar on Facebook/Meta-Hari. I'm always lurking with my correcting "pencil" handy. The world is carelessly worded. Someone must come to its aid—the mantle of Mr. Walker.

As a matter of fact, I suppose this column is a letter. Give this a try: clip it and put it in an envelope. Mail it to someone and see if it starts a correspondence. It has my "Forever" stamp. Take a letter.

Sincerely,
Todd R. Nelson

Train Time

"I wanted to know where the trains were going."

—Dennis Hopper on his Kansas childhood.

WE WERE ON THE AMTRAK DOWNEASTER in Dover, New Hampshire before the question was asked by an eighth grade wag: "Are we, like, there yet?"

"Nope."

It's a long way to Boston, and we actually sought to make it take a little longer by approaching our destination by rail on that year's eighth grade class trip. Sometimes, it's good to go the slow way. It's a test of one's attention span and powers of observation.

I appreciate trains. In fact, it's too bad you can't take a train all the way from Bangor to Boston anymore. So, we had to begin the railroad portion of our trip at the present northern terminus of passenger service: Portland. Whereas "fast" used to be the speed of a steam train, nowadays diesel train time feels sluggish. But when you travel by train, you see a few 19th century vistas go by the window, and that was part of the point. We've all been down the Maine Turnpike to Boston, but the rail thoroughfare makes you think of a different era of transportation, goods, services, and community, and observing the former landscape.

We arrived, town by town, via the backdoor, via a right-of-way that has probably changed little since it was established. We clickety-clacked through town squares and depots new and old, and new-old—replica stations complete with old-fashioned railway clocks. In some ways, might this be a kind of "core sampling" of history, human settlement of the eastern corridor, the growth of suburbs, the decline of New England industries and the ascendancy of others, the decay and rebuilding of urban centers? Our iron horse bore us into the past.

Here were old iron bridges in Dover, abandoned mills in Saco, beautiful farms (dairy and Christmas tree) with exurbs pressing their boundaries, and constant fluctuation between cleared land and young forests. We passed clam-flats with clam diggers hard at work; salt marshes hard by new condominiums south of Portland. Clearly in some communities we rolled through, the tracks used to be outside of town. Now they bisect neighborhoods. We passed steeples at the front door of towns (we could see Sunday mass just letting out at St. Mary's in Dover, New Hampshire) and smokestacks at the backdoor; town parks and salvage yards. And then, finally, the thicket of rail yards, suburban backyards, and triple-decker apartment houses on the final slow creep to Boston's North Station. We were there.

The railroads brought standardization of time in the United States. To the eighth grade trip, the train ride brought leisure and a certain suspension of time. We couldn't go any faster, or stop any less frequently, than the Downeaster's timetable. Other aspects of the trip had a similar slowing effect. A museum, for instance, gives you pause. Unlike, say, the Discovery channel, the displays at the Museum of Fine Arts don't change every few seconds. One becomes reacquainted with a long view, really seeing things because they don't flicker on and off at a predetermined interval. Whether it was the Egyptian statuary or the Fillmore concert posters from the "Summer of Love," the exhibits spoke to us of our attention span, and ourselves as watchers.

It's true too of a city like Boston, the "city on a hill" laid out on old cow paths as opposed to modern urban planning and the logical grid of an industrial age city such as Chicago—"player with Railroads and the Nation's Freight Handler." The juxtaposition is glaring when such a city collides with a modern population's growth and need for transportation and sanitation, scrambling to align its infrastructure with the future—the big dig, for example. We were guests on its front doorstep.

Are we there yet? As Gertrude Stein said of Oakland, "There's no there there." But we saw plenty of "there"—or at least there was plenty to see, if you knew what to look for. Next year, perhaps we'll take a different old time route. In the age of sail, the Downeaster was a ship, and it left our bay and approached Boston by sea carrying bricks, lumber, ice, and fish. The sea: now that's an old thoroughfare. I'm, like, totally there.

The Man in
the Photo

I AM THE ARCHIVIST of our family story: all the old photos of individuals and reunions, the genealogy trees, the family Bibles, and even the DNA evidence of origins in our global, migratory arc; who we are, in a narrative and biological sense.

One photo has always intrigued me. Unlike any other, it gives a tantalizing clue as to what "we" *did*. Starting in 1906, the Nelsons took care to photograph their family reunions, take formal portraits, and, as cameras improved, commemorative snapshots in front of their houses and on celebratory occasions: graduation, the WWI armistice, etc. We very purposefully recorded our corporate and individual identity. Still do. Then there is the black and white photo of my great grandfather standing with coworkers in a machine shop, simply labeled, "Tool Room, King Construction Co. Tonawanda, NY." He looks at the camera as if shyly addressing the photographer. It was just another inauspicious day at work. Nothing to see here, folks. But he was peering into the future.

Great grandfather was in the first generation born in this country. His parents, Jeannie Callum and Alexander Nelson, came from Glasgow to Toronto on their honeymoon in 1867, settling near Buffalo. Other family may have preceded them. Alexander was a carpenter and railroad conductor. His father had been a plowman, near Dunbar, on the east coast of Scotland. For four generations, the American Nelsons lived in a tightly conscribed circle around Tonawanda, I discovered through census records and lore. Many of them still do, which I only learned recently—cousins I've never met.

DNA is a remarkable narrative device. Mine reached back farther than the Scottish census and church records to the deep biological Nelson record. We were Scandinavians, perhaps Vikings, before residing in Scotland for a few centuries. I envision Nils Neilson the Red scouting landfall on the coast of Caithness from his longboat in, say, the 12th century. A millennium later—off to America. . . . for a while.

DNA also clarified this photo. I did not know what happened to my father's uncle and cousins. Like a laboratory detective, my DNA test found them. Family names had changed, and yet a first cousin who had also done DNA testing closed the gap. Suddenly, I was in correspondence with a lost Nelson—descendant of great uncle David. One thing led to another, explanatory details on both sides. Cousins knew family details and stories that I didn't, verifying the connection. And I shared the photos of the oldest generations to be photographed.

"There was a grandfather who carved wooden horses," Magin, my new-found cousin said. A mystery—solved by a link to the Herschell Carousel factory, founded by a fellow Scot, in Tonawanda, New York, where great grandfather James spent his whole career. Herschell bought King Construction, and the tool room. Now a museum, its website listed all his employment dates and residential addresses, even his spouse. Subsequent emails with the director confirmed the match. The company made thousands of carousels sold all over the country. The man in my photo was the wooden horse man. And there's a Herschell carousel in Maine that's destined to be relocated to Orrington. I wonder if James ever signed his work? I hope to see.

James had two sons: Robert James and David Charles Nelson. Robert James became an accountant and had a son, Robert Colby, pictured in another old photo on the lap of his great grandmother, Jeannie, the wizened matriarch. She was the last Nelson to speak with a Glasgow accent. Robert Colby became a journalist, left Tonawanda, and had a son, Todd Robin. He became a teacher and writer, took great interest in the family's Scottish roots, visited the old country several times, even learned to play the bagpipes—a profound zealotry. He had a daughter, Ariel Rose, who went to George Stevens Academy in Blue Hill and then got a BA at Glasgow School of Art, the city of her ancestors, and is now in Aberdeen at Gray's School of Art. That's five generations worth of what "we" do.

It's a long journey from the slums of the east end of Glasgow in 1867 to graduate school in Aberdeen in 2018, a mental circumnavigation much farther than the physical route through New York, five generations, and back. I expect an Aberdeen accent to join the family soon.

The Lost Poem

I HAD LOVED POETRY FOR YEARS—poems that sounded cool, had "deep inner meanings," powerful rhetoric, clinched a theme, or simply had a beguiling, musical, humorous, unique voice or beauty. I was, in fact, an English major, studying poetry in college. Already a dedicated academic reader, I was also archiving poems that spoke to my heart and personal experiences—my anthology of poems.

Then I found a poem that changed everything. It captured my heart; witnessed and gave tribute to my experience and summarized my inner, youthful, amorous longings. It was a balm, even years after the heartbreak. It explained who I had been, as a 16-year-old smitten with an older girl who had a Shakespearian-romance name. She was my heartthrob, the emotional weather of August on which summer pivoted. The backdrop was a summer cottage on a north country river, laughter and canoodling.

The surprise poem also explained to me who I had become—a maturing college student with a modicum of hindsight. And it spoke to who I would become. I can still feel its tipping me into a new realm of appreciating poetry thanks to its psychic purchase. It crept up on me. It infiltrated. It changed everything I thought about what poems do. It was a love poem directed backward in time, toward the companion and lover who had made summer a golden moment for the poet—love in hindsight, that is. Like mine. I needed its therapy.

I read it once. Then I lost it. It lay hidden somewhere within the bound volumes of *The New Yorker* magazine I had been perusing in the college library stacks. I could not remember the author nor title. I recalled only the last line: "I needed to have loved you. I needed to have told you so." It was what I needed to be able to say.

I began a quest to retrieve the poem that had retrieved a whole summer of memory for me. I knew the range of bound volumes in which I had seen it, but when exactly? I could visualize its shape on the page, and that last line haunting me like the lost chord. I wanted its resonance back. It said something I didn't know how to say, about a story I wanted to be true.

Most importantly, I wanted its swelling feeling. I remembered reading that last line, the finale for images of a summer romance encapsulated in the poem's amber. I remembered its point of view, questions, sense of loss, a tug of longing, and a recovery that I understood personally—and needed. The poem shared my point of view, spoke to me, for me, as me.

Eureka. It took years, but when I found it my emotional cavities filled. "A Kindness," by William Dickey, was indeed restorative.

"Where did we stop?" he wrote, and then rehearsed the thrilling explorations and discoveries in a summer relationship. Dickey spoke to me with the exact imagery of my own memories, and the synthesis of their meaning. "You stripped into that glare of live gold," he wrote. It could have been my line.

It was like living in gold to try to touch you.
It was as if you were day.

His summer was my summer of love. The imagery matched, the feelings matched, and even the trick of memory matched—"none of this is true, but will you let me have it, imaginary?" His words worked better than my own to reanimate my past. I too wanted my memory to be "a bush of grown flame." It's what a good poem is capable of.

Even tonight, decades later, "A Kindness" summons a simultaneous pang and an honest appreciation—it speaks to who I was and who I have become, no longer young but understanding better now than at 16 what the light was like.

> *It is a kindness you can do me, to have been there*
> *at the center of summer, yourself the attack of summer,*
> *and to have made all that light out of being young.*

Three years after the summer "of the poem," I was to meet my wife, who was described in many more poems that would encapsulate my maturing heart. In fact, ours was a courtship-by-poetry. She too was "at the center of summer," a subsequent August, an endless summer; aflame. She wore a red *Yes, The New Yorker* T-shirt. I was all in.

Now, as fresh poems accrue, I make sure not to misplace them. With the lost poem, I began the verse anthology that I call my life. And I am still the boy who had the summer infatuation, the young man who lost its lyric verse companionship, and the maturing man who is learning the love lessons of them all.

The New Year Heffalump Count

THE ANNUAL COUNT OF LOCAL HEFFALUMPS is made more difficult when there is no snow on the ground. The received wisdom is that counting is based on footprints, not actual sightings (rare), and heffalumps prefer not to step in mud, clay, sand, and other trackable ground. Snow it is, based on the literature. Even a mere dusting will do for us trackers.

And literature on the heffalump is scant. At times, it seems its existence is more legend or fantasy than fact, a creature born of fiction. Nonetheless, there remains a dedicated group of researchers who assemble yearly for the New Year count, somewhat like the Audubon Christmas bird count in which volunteer birdwatchers nationwide enumerate species and numbers to assess the health of an avian population.

I have a few techniques to share. My dogs accompanied me on this year's count. Since the heffalump is scentless and secretive, Betty and Lola were more companions for me than effective scouts or heffalump trackers. Squirrels, on the other hand, are another matter. Within a few steps into the woods, the red squirrels were scolding us from branches on high and the gray (now lumbering, thanks to their pilfering of my bird feeder larder—why even call it bird seed?) had retreated to their nests and resumed slumber.

I think this favors the heffalump, a shy and slow-moving critter who prefers forest silence and a meditative gait. To count a heffalump, one must attempt to *be a heffalump*. This requires curiosity, a focus and observation of the minute details of the forest floor, the changes in ground covering, debris, leaf mulch, and obstructions like fallen logs and large rocks. Watch the change from path-worn dirt, to mossy carpet, to puddle, to reindeer lichen. Step softly, pausing with each lift and plant of the foot, and observe the little neighborhoods of beetles and salamanders and worms and ants. Pay special attention to footprints, especially one's own.

This is not so much a hunt as a *meander*. Normal purposefulness is a hindrance; aimlessness is a helpful tactic. It's good to circle a large tree or glacial erratic or even a patch of hayfield several times, walking in the same place each time so as not to print one's own prints repeatedly. One might even begin tracking oneself. It has happened. And just when you recognize the repetition, you also recognize the new line of thinking you've commenced. *No path is the same twice,* you think—a heffalump has successfully drawn you in.

And it's interesting to look around for heffalump burrows, nests, mobile homes, or hollows. Any large rock, hollow tree, or collection of branches up high in the firs could be a suitable home; any unfamiliar tent, sleeping bag, or camp cabin too. Like the cuckoo, they may also occupy the homes of fellow woodland species as if they were their own, saving construction and space—but this is an area of research in search of a researcher.

Other research topics beckon: migratory habits, food preferences, rearing the young, and trumpeting calls—mating, feeding, warning and alerts; favorite karaoke tunes and pack identifiers.

Packs? Do heffalumps congregate in packs, like other familiar woodland critters? Some of the beehive ransacking blamed on Maine Black Bears, may in fact be caused by heffalumps. Their predilection for honey is well established in the literature. Haycorns (or acorns) are similarly imagined to attract heffalumps, though they weary of the effort it takes to collect them. Heffalumps encourage bees to do their honey-gathering. Smart.

A.A. Milne is, of course, the preeminent heffalump expert—see his research from 100-acre wood if in doubt. It's the original text.

Alas—no sightings, today; no tracks, no sonic glints, no photos. One might think our count was not a success. That, however, would miss the point. The experience is productive even without tangible evidence—and what constitutes *tangible,* anyway? Elusive though it may be; defiant of detection, the heffalump is not entirely *undetectable.* It all depends on your filter. This creature tends to show up when least expected, when least searched for. In fact, it helps to turn off the searching, intellectual pursuit to stand the best chance of a sighting. It reminds me of my perennial desire to see a bear, and the fact that they appear when least expected. In fact, I've come to see that this annual count works best as an imagination index. Are we alive to the "willing suspension of our disbelief?" Hope so. This year's count was a big affirmative, even without leaving the house. It augurs well for the new year.

How Poetry
Ruined My Life

NOW AS I WAS YOUNG AND EASY, my childhood was ruined
by beautiful writing and high-minded values and verbal expression, and I blame it all on poetry. For years, my parents left
this dangerous, unstable writing lying around the house in plain
sight. It was, alas, the era before parent advisory labels. Mom and
Dad left poems where unsuspecting children could find them.
For birthday cards, there were poetic quotes. For the solution to
every torment, from mere doldrums of summer to heartbreak
and adolescent angst, there were quotes from poems.

My early years were imbued with the sense that language was
the most precious thing in the world; that putting the right words
in the right order was a virtuous life work; that finding power,
and style, and beauty in language was the highest calling—all
telegraphed to us kids by poems taped on the fridge and liberal
quoting of verse. Poetry, it was clear, was the fount of wisdom,
insight, and memorable, gorgeous expression. Even today, when
I pluck a few, cherished anthologies from my shelf, it starts a
flood of memory and feeling. Deeply embedded lines come to
the fore like old acquaintances.

I still have the *Leaves of Grass* that Dad gave me for Christmas in ninth grade. "Whitman loved much that you love—beauty, openness, honesty, freedom, nature. Inside here is his 'Song of the Open Road.' You are entering your open road years. Demand much of them; give them fully of yourself and you will have come to terms with being."

Dad felt obliged to convey pathos and meaning at every opportunity. How about a new bicycle for Christmas? Nope. But I bet I can now find a poem about it. By twelfth grade, I only wanted one thing for Christmas: *The Complete Poems of e.e. cummings.* Powerful words and emotions had infected my soul.

My paperback copy of Oscar Williams *Pocket Book of Modern Verse* was a constant companion for two years of high school English. It's here on my shelf. Mr. Walker gave excruciatingly precise tests of memory based on that book. I still recall hours of poring over titles and poets, ready to identify any snippet of verse for tests covering 40 poems—the power of the poems, the power of recollecting them. Phrases from "Walker poems" still come to mind: "A poem should not mean but be," "Imaginary gardens with real toads in them," "had anything been wrong we would certainly have heard." There. I've shared a poetry scavenger hunt.

Try taking a walk in the woods without Wordsworth or Frost accompanying you! The woods are always "lovely, dark and deep"—Oooo that comma! Try taking in a winter landscape without hearing in the sound of the wind "the nothing that is not there, and the nothing that is." There's always a certain "slant of light" that must be appreciated or described. It makes the world a word-scape ripe for shaping and appreciation beyond the prosaic.

Inside the tent of poetry (metaphor alert!) I found a world of imagination ("'Twas brillig"), nature's beauty (My senior yearbook quote: "Gie me a' the spark o' nature's fire, that's a' the learnin' I desire,"), and even environmentalism ("It is only a little planet, but oh how beautiful it is"). Poetry had an answer for everything and beckoned to "a helluva good universe next door: let's go." It gauged human psyche and history and potential all in cadence and rhyme: "We fray into the future, rarely wrought save in the tapestries of afterthought."

The pernicious influence of an even greater range of poets was cemented in place in college: I was an English major. I read the old and middle English, Shakespearian, Romantic, Victorian, and modern British and American poets before settling on T.S. Eliot for my thesis topic. Senior year was "Four Quartets." And what does one do with a B.A. in English? Teach poetry, of course. So I did. Misery.

Now my bookshelves groan with anthologies of all kinds. I can locate a poem on any theme—from running to golf to automobiles; guitar riffs to swimming lessons; geometry to thermodynamics; ants to Zulus. Nothing exceeds the grasp of the poetic imagination. Everything good, lasting, meaningful can be found in a poem.

In my professional life, I once had the privilege of interviewing Billy Collins, U.S. poet laureate. "Poetry is the result," he said, "of taking an obsessive interest in language and finding that using language in a certain way can express what otherwise cannot be expressed. The history of poetry is the only surviving history we have of human emotion. It is the history of the human heart. There is no other one. Without poetry, we would be deprived of the emotional companionship of our ancestors." No pressure, Billy.

There is now no walk for me that is not Thoreauvian; no day not filled with metaphor; no moment not experienced metaphysically or transcendentally, "beauty and truth, truth beauty," everywhere. I cannot see "a certain slant of light," or hear the winter wind without "hearing the nothing that is not there and the nothing that is"—the world *is* words. The "Little lame balloon man" augurs spring for me. The poet is the "priest of the invisible," or an alien from inner space. "Poetry is the bill and coo of sex," saith the poet. Erotica! It is a burden to be so dominated by great writing. Mommas, don't let your babies grow up to be English majors, though they will "come to terms with being"—like that'll pay the bills.

My kids have been affected too, receiving poems as birthday letters or sundry quote barrages. "Happy birthday, honey. Have I sent you this one by Wendell Berry, recently? William Stafford! Sharon Olds! Naomi Shihab Nye." The word, the word, the word. Always gotta quote; share something pithy and succinct; passing along meaning, and feeling, and beautiful expression in other people's words. It's not enough to merely state a point—it must always have maximum possible resonance. Emotional companionship indeed. Yup, poetry made me the pitiful, empathic, romantic, Keatsian, truth-seeking, beauty-seeking, beatnik, transcendental, articulate man I am today—such as I was, such as I would become. "Horseman pass by."

Herein lie the words of Eliot, Yeats, Cummings, Burns, Wilbur, Stevens, MacLeish, Dickinson, Sandburg, Frost, Keats, Carroll, Thomas.

Junkyard Thoughts

"In the car's dream the road goes on forever."

—Susan Mitchell, "The Road"

I DON'T RECALL THE MODELS, but I do remember the way the old abandoned cars in the orchard smelled. And I could probably still find my way to that wooded junkyard, so vividly etched in my recollections of ages nine to twelve, if the apple trees haven't grown too thick or the surrounding tall pines succumbed to tract housing. The cars smelled like steamer trunks stored in an attic, like old leather shoes, like newspapers; old, worn, comfortable and a mite decayed. Or vintage, with a musty patina.

It was a pastoral junkyard, if such a thing is possible. You crossed through Jeff's yard, jumped the stone wall and took the path across the field and along the woods. The collection of twenty or so cars, beyond an old farmhouse, was a profound discovery and for a while a fanciful haunt. I remember, on mostly sunny days, exploring the rusty hulks of sedans and trucks that languished under apple trees, their hoods and trunks sprung, the doors askew, paint the texture of sandpaper.

We imagined they had been driven to their resting place, carefully parked, then left in their forlorn ranks simply awaiting further usefulness with the best intention of repair. At least used for parts? Not sold for scrap! This parking lot of relics was certainly a playground for roaming nine-year-olds and nesting place for mice, birds, and squirrels. It was sad to think of them as abandoned by the dictates of the enigmatic, arbitrary numbers rolled up on the odometers while some of their fortunate siblings no doubt endure as prized rides in July 4th parades, with flags and bunting on their fenders.

Most of their windows were intact, their bodywork only slightly rumpled. We admired their hood ornaments, like fleet figureheads in corrupted chrome, and tried mightily to release the rusty bolts and collect them. When we found a rearview mirror still in place it meant we could sit inside and realistically "drive" them. Atop the bouncy spring seats, plush thrones to my cronies and me, higher than barber chairs, we twisted steering wheels that seemed as big around as the balloon tires on our bicycles—so different in scale from the Ford Falcon back in the driveway at my house.

So, we would pretend to drag race, or coast along the highway, watching out the rearview mirror for the Highway Patrol, or be the Highway Patrol in hot pursuit. Or the chauffeur. Or soup up the engine by pretending to tinker with mysterious wires and bolts. On a few of the old cars, our feet would reach the pedals and we could practice double clutching with "three on the tree." We learned the concept of flooring it. Or we could just listen to the bees work the orchard and wonder archeologically about past drivers.

My 15-year-old daughter will remember my Ford-F150 similarly for its decrepitude and smell and her first lessons in shifting its "four on the floor." She already refers to it as ready for junking and I admit it is taking on many of the characteristics of those wrecks of recollection. It's certainly got the smell. But I prefer to think of its rust as a patina. And I relish its comfortable shabbiness, which makes it, in my mind, more useful.

It has been two years since I bought it, having looked past the rust-pocked panels and hood, torn driver's seat, cheesy floorboards and malfunctioning radio. It is the oldest vehicle I have ever owned. The engine runs well, with coaxing and patience. It sounds good (but what do I know about engine timbre); has low mileage for the model year (but what do I know about the kind of miles they were); was a good model year (but what do I know). Four-wheel drive (Location, location, location).

My first truck. The price was right. One owner, who lowered that price as we drove in the driveway. And the seller called her "her." Ah, character. In our neck of the woods, everyone seems to call trucks "her." So I began the relationship. I softened the presence of the gun rack in the cab with my Super-Soaker pump-action squirt gun, hung fuzzy dice on the rearview mirror, and started pumping money into generally expected, but unforeseen, renovations.

The hydraulic brake lines went first and, since I can still only pretend to tinker with such maintenance, Harry Webber had to replace them. Then the shocks. I was driving her up the Castine road and the heavy-duty shocks took leave of the frame mounts and almost sent me on a loop-the-loop while I rode back down to Harry's garage for rewelding. Time for a new gas tank as well. Then brake linings.

But what I most appreciate about my truck is the lack of fuss, like an old sofa. It is fully depreciated and derelict in appearance, so it can finally be fully used. Dirt, seaweed, manure for the garden, trash, recycling, dumpster gleanings, firewood, lumber, the wet dog—all ride in the back. We have achieved the honest heart of a vehicle's life mission—beyond engineering, advertising, and lifestyle associations: to connect two points, real and imagined.

Mechanical problems have quieted down over the winter. Perhaps she'll hold her own for a while. But pothole season approaches. And I sense the impending cost-benefit analysis of an old car owner—of the orchard cars' owners. At what point does full usefulness become too pricey? For now, I hate to reduce a vehicle with a personal pronoun, and a patina, to such a logical equation. The best connection between two points, as any driver knows, is often the most circuitous.

Now We Are Six—or 16

OUR DAUGHTER CAN STILL BE CALLED a young teacher, still in the early years of her career in the family business. Like her mother, she teaches kindergarten. She has more wisdom than her experience justifies—certainly more than my own at the equivalent stage of my school teaching career.

It is August, and after a summer of adventures abroad she is preparing for the new school year, enacting all the things imagined and planned during her hiatus. I know that rhythm well. And yet I am also remembering the close of the prior year, her first in a new school.

Last June, she sent a photo of the gifts she had given her students: an individual book in which she had written each child's accomplishments, and a copy of *Now We Are Six* by A.A. Milne. That was the book we gave her as she turned kindergarten-plus-one. She knew that June 8, the last day, would be a boundary and a benchmark; a destination as well as an embarkation point for new shores and sequel stories.

Awareness of the journey and achievement includes a tender pivot that hopes for stasis. It can't be, even as Milne subtly and ruefully hints:

But now I am Six, I'm as clever as clever,
So I think I'll be six now for ever and ever.

Who doesn't want the ability to press pause? Her kids had been zany for weeks. "Dad!" she wrote, "they're driving me nuts." They had somehow become "six" prior to the (artificial) deadline and were feeling their oats. Chaos and consternation, uncomfortable as they might be, are usually the signs of growth, sloughing off an old skin and pulling on the new—with brighter colors and crazy hair days. Toss the tight curriculum timetable out the window. Engineering punctiliousness does not apply to child development—heck, to human growth and maturity. But she knew that.

She coached her class parents on managing the end of kindergarten and the transition to first grade—managing the emotions bubbling up in the kids and themselves.

"Observe the story your kids are experiencing; know that it is *their* age appropriate version of events, and be their experienced guide. Don't mistake their experience for your own," she wrote.

A year with Ms. Nelson is a voyage of discovery ("Like when we got in our cardboard boats and navigated past hydrothermal vents, mermaids, mersloths, and wild things!" she reminded them at the closing ceremony), improvisation, hard tasks, and jubilant accomplishments. It is field trips to the Exploratorium, the local firehouse; mapmaking, oceangoing voyages, and excursions to the zoo. It is sloth time and pirate day and performing *Where the Wild Things Are* for the whole school. It is speaking in Spanish . . . and kindness and tolerance. And it is laughter and celebration.

Is this just an end-of-year theme? Seems to me it's a good back-to-school pivot as well.

In a subsequent video, a massive classroom clean-up was in progress complete with Led Zeppelin soundtrack. Nothing like a little "Ramble On" to get the cubbies spic and span.

It's a melancholy rite, removing a year's worth of pictures and graphics from any school classroom. These are the singular, sacred hieroglyphics of the unique inhabitants. The walls look forlorn. The memories and accomplishments archived in humble drawings and hard-won stories must go home with the writers and artists who made them. The palette is wiped; the stage is struck. It must be fresh for the next artists, actors, and corps de ballet. Woe unto the teacher who simply restores last year's posters to the bulletin boards. It must be preparation for renewal. "Next year," Hilary said, "I'm going to put the classroom library in the very center of the room." Reading is power in Classroom 2.0.

The teacher too will be fresh and renewed. Not content to repeat the same curriculum or activity, because the fresh faces *are* the curriculum and they deserve a brand-new script, just as Hilary did when she went to first grade, age six, all those classrooms and teachers ago; when her own young teachers and even younger parents affirmed her milestones. Just as—one hopes—any incoming student or teacher can expect in the rollout of a new year, now that we are six—or 16, or 60. I'm looking forward to Wild Things—the sequel.

The Mummer
Motif

The Old Padstow May Day Carol goes like this:

Unite and unite and let us all unite,
For summer is acome unto day,
And whither we are going we all will unite,
In the merry morning of May.

These traditional words augur many things. A traditional May Day song from the English villages of yore, it invites us to gather together at a certain time to dance, sing, and hope—that spring rains have worked their alchemy on the roots of winter, that crops will flourish, that our labors will produce bounty, that the village will thrive in our time, and that St. George will slay the dragon. The English farmers who created the Morris dances, Mummer and May pole traditions still followed in many communities, lived according to a time and rhythm quite different from our own—but we are their heirs. You could feel it when our 1-2 graders did their Mummers play on Friday. St. George won again.

Schools are some of the last places in contemporary society where the village rituals and agrarian calendar persist, at least as an echo of olden times. Whereas, in ages past, our fellowship would focus on commerce and land stewardship, we now celebrate the life of learning and waymarks of childhood. Quaint, charming, fitting, and time honored. So, here in the "merry morning of May" what have we planted? What will we reap? What time is it?

If you ask a preschooler for their definition of time, some amazing concepts flourish. It tends to be attached to doing something. Time isn't an abstraction, it's an action. "It means it's time to be finished with your picture," a preschooler once told me. "When it's time to leave." Or, "Day time, meeting area time, snack time," says another. In the larger culture, time tends to be a line. It unfurls as the crow flies, from A to B, young to old, season-to-season, hour-to-hour. But there are other ways of expressing it that might be worth considering: a spiral, a thought, an immersion, or the oscillation of a preschooler awaiting snack time.

We have the anecdotal research to suggest that time spent foraging for the best berry patches, fishing spots, fairy gardens, and even hours spent plying the waters of local ponds or Blodgett woods, is a great predictor of creative, ingenious, fulfilled human beings passing formative years in play. In part, this is due to a different declination of time, and I propose a new name for it: mytho-time. These are the activities of minutes and hours not counted in minutes and hours, the passage of discoveries and accomplishments of the hand, heart, and soul, not the external tick-tock that regiments so much of modern life. It's the languorous turn of the page in a summer book, and the internal passage from questioning to synthesizing to knowing—and knowing that you know. It is painting at the easel time, or wood-working time, or meandering in the woods time. It is immersion in thought and feeling and observing that is timeless time. This kind of time is of the essence of things.

Our Westward Migration

"WE USED TO COME FROM MOOSE RIVER," I'm fond of saying, "we're away for a few generations, and now we're back." Sort of. Maine ancestry is a point of pride and privilege. When my Holden, Colby, and Churchill ancestors came to the Moose River Valley in the early 1700s, it took fortitude and grit to make a go of it. Of course, in many ways that hasn't changed. Mainers do whatever it takes to make a go of it.

My great grandfather, Walter Welch Colby, was born in Moose River in 1861. His father, Spencer, a blacksmith and son of Ambrose Colby, took the family west in a covered wagon following the Civil War. He had served in the Maine 14th regiment. With his wife, Josephine Churchill, and their six children, including a young Walter, they settled for a number of years in Grand Rapids, Michigan and had more children, some of whom later married into local families. Then in 1870 they pushed on to Nebraska, with an older brother, Philander Colby. They were looking for better farmland to make a go of it during the land rush era. Spencer and Josephine had a total of thirteen children, which would give me a lot of extant cousins across the country.

They wrote letters from Michigan back to the family in Moose River in 1869. "I am making maple sugar this spring," Spencer wrote. "We live four miles from Philander's. His family is all well and he is making sugar. I have two acres of winter wheat sown and intend to plant four or five acres of corn and a few potatoes. This is a good country for wheat, corn, and grass and stock raising and a great place to raise fruit such as apples, peaches, pears, plums, and some cherries and most anything you may want to raise."

Spencer also advised his brother, Helon, to come west. "It will not cost you more than $100 to come out west and look around for a month or so and I think you would conclude not to buy at Moose River. I am rather poor but you could not get me to go back there. I do not say that Michigan is the best place in the world, but you can go into any of the new western states."

And that's exactly what he and Philander did.

They went to Marquette, Nebraska, had more children, who married other farm families in the area. Spencer revisited Maine in 1913, the year before he died. (Josephine predeceased him by seven years.) He finally lived with Walter's family and my grandmother would have known him for several years in her childhood. Spencer's memorial service in 1914 was summarized in the local paper. "The funeral services were attended by the few remaining members of Putnam Post, G. A. R., of which the deceased was a member, who assembled at the hall and marched as an escort in a body. Mr. Colby had been so long identified with the history of Marquette that he had become one of its oldest, remaining citizens, and out of respect the business houses closed during the service." He's buried in Richland Cemetery.

It's been a long way back. In my generation, we've lived in five states and both coasts. This too is an American story, not moving for better dirt and pasture but for professional opportunity.

Perhaps they're equivalent. But in the arc of the greater Colby-Nelson family, we are clearly people who will move. There's a pioneer strain, and a modicum of settler. And a newfound sense of place in the greater story.

Our family photographic record truly begins with this photo of Walter taken in Nebraska. It's the earliest photo we own, from any side of our clan. Another Nebraska photo, taken a few years later, shows my grandmother, June Marie Colby, who I knew well, standing with her parents and sister Josephine in their backyard in Marquette. It is circa 1920. Walter's wife, Minnie Melvina Cudney, came from Iowa and lived on her family's farm, next door to the Colbys.

In another photo, June has a pony. In the 1910 census, Walter is listed as a laborer; Minnie, as a nurse. Photos concur. He always has the same gaze, young or old: direct; a stare into that flat horizon line. He died in 1931, living with my grandmother June in Tonawanda, New York, and is buried in the family plot back in Marquette, far from the cemetery with his Holden, Colby, and Churchill kin in Moose River. June was married by then, and my father was a year old.

I often contemplate Walter's journey and what he must have seen in his lifetime: from Moose River to Michigan to the land rush western frontier and back to industrial Buffalo and a final seven years working at Remington. It's almost too much to conceive of, in the heady westward expansion of an American century, until you consider the present pace of change, and the photos we're now sharing with our descendants.

The Myrmidons Take Ripogenus Dam

A reflection on the 42nd anniversary of an epic campaign

MY CHILDHOOD GANG GATHERED at Hurley's pond for raft voyages along its great gray-green greasy banks. We had an instinctual urge to mess around on things that (modestly) float; and with mud, and sticks. We could be Ulysses, Huck, Captains Hook or Nemo, Vikings, and swashbucklers. A child with a plank or a stick is an empire of fierce imaginative possibilities. Everyone needs to have had a raft, been a swashbuckler, felt heroic, and made a brave connection with adventure.

My favorite raft came many years later and was one I shared with my wife, Lesley. It was constructed of imagination and early marital bravery while Lesley and I were leading a wilderness camp trip. Just the two of us and a dozen 13-year-old boys hiked from Mt. Katahdin down the Appalachian Trail for 10 days, culminating in an unanticipated raft epic on a remote, off-trail Maine pond.

It all started on a sunny day hiking the steep, rocky backside of the great Katahdin. We were treated to a rare view of the Atlantic from the summit, picked cranberries and blueberries from the tundra-like lawns on the mountain's alpine shoulders, and lolled above Chimney Pond. Crows and hawks soared on the updrafts of valley air. Our gang was being convened.

We were on constant alert for bears and moose as we trod southward on the Baxter Park trails the next day. John McPhee calls the expectant moments of yearning to spot a moose as having "the stillness of a moose intending to appear." A dozen teenage boys, transfixed with the desire to see a moose, or the ambivalent wish to spot a bear, from a distance, can actually hush. Our moose—a cow bolting across the trail and bobbing into the woods—finally appeared. But a moose's fleeing rump is not a sighting to tell stories about—important in a trip the gang wished to call "an exploit."

We had five days trekking beside clear lakes and cool, mossy streams; deep, dark pine woods and wild meadows, eventually arriving on the shores of Chesuncook Pond, a day's walk from our destination: Ripogenus Dam on the Golden Road.

We had left the trail at the end of Rainbow Lake and bush-whacked through the forest and acres of raspberry-covered logging sites—bear country—to get to Chesuncook. Released from the rote walking of the trail, far from other hikers or camp-grounds, our imaginations transposed Maine woods to magical forests and our purpose from simple hike to quest. The bush-whacking, navigating by compass, by instinct, and by lookout from an occasional tall pine, had whetted our appetite for der-ring-do. What a finale it would be to build a raft and sail across the narrows between the two bays of Chesuncook Pond!

We pitched our tents on the bouldered shore and ate a last macaroni and cheese dinner. The sun lodged in the pines to the west and a loon warbled tales of brave Ulysses to our swashbuckling crew.

We awoke to torrential rain. Turn back? No. By God, we would not be denied our exploit.

The boys hauled jackstraw fir trees out of the woods for a deck lashed atop our buoyant sleeping bag pads. We would float our packs across by swimming behind, pushing. Why not get soaked in the process—all the more heroic! The mission: dry clothes on the opposite side. Our strongest swimmers were the engine. We stepped into the waves. 'Twas then little Chip noticed the leeches.

"Swim for it men!" I shouted, launching the raft. The Myrmidons hove into action, kicking furiously for the far shore. The battle cry went up: "Ripogenus Dam!"

I drew my claymore from its scabbard; Lesley fit an arrow of desire to her longbow. The leeches lurked behind trees and laurel bushes on the shore. They outnumbered us, though they were no taller than a bull moose and seemed tentative about venturing into the froth of our withdrawal across this backwoods Hellespont. The vigor of my sword strokes and Lesley's sure bead had them stymied. Warning shots o'er head convinced them: settle for a standoff. Then Lesley and I slipped into the gentle Chesuncook waters, dimpled by the warm July rain, and gracefully paddled to the far side. We had achieved our raft exploit. And the odyssey continues.

Pool Party

I'M NO WILDLIFE EXPERT, but I was worrying about the effect of the summer drought on my woodland friends. The deer looked parched, the raccoons a bit frazzled, and the foxes were dragging their tails. I had a remedy in mind: sharing the kiddie pool I had stored in the rafters of the garage. Obvious solution.

I dragged it out back of the house and stuck the hose in to start filling. Then I positioned my trail camera to keep an eye on the new neighborhood wildlife pool . . . and imagined the pool party I was inviting.

Day one I noticed a couple of does and two fawns putting their little deer lips down to the water and getting a tasty drink. They lingered for a while and melted back into the undergrowth. You're welcome!

Day two, my trail camera recorded a skunk trundling past in the wee hours of the morning. She poked her head over the side and took a sip. Then, thankfully, kept walking and digging grubs out of my lawn. The fragrance of her presence lingered for a while.

Day three was the game changer. I looked out back and noticed a construction of twigs and bark beside the pool. It looked like a carefully assembled lifeguard chair. Sure enough, there on the trail camera was a picture of a raccoon sitting atop the perch he had built, a whistle lanyard around his neck, his nose slathered with what I can only assume was sunscreen. SPF furry woodland creature. He jauntily hung an elbow over the armrest and peered intently down on the pool, awaiting customers.

By day four, the pool filled with tree frogs and a few grass snakes. They seemed pleased with the water temperature and shared the space without rancor. That night, something else happened. A sign had been installed: "Pool Rules." All two of them.

Don't make a mess.

If you make a mess, clean it up—without being asked by the lifeguard. The raccoon had brought standards to the pool.

Day five seemed to be the threshold of a whole new dynamic: the rabbits arrived, and the raccoon added rule #3: "No roughhousing in the deep end."

"What's roughhousing?" asked an annoying red squirrel.

"If you have to ask. . . . Oh, just listen for the whistle," said the raccoon. "I'll let you know." Red retreated to his spruce limb.

The whistle sounded. "Buddy check!" yelled raccoon. The mice and voles scurried to their partners and held up a paw.

Then one day two beavers arrived. "Seems kind of puny," they muttered. "How about a little reconstruction?" they said to raccoon.

"What did you have in mind?" he answered.

"Bigger. It's what we do," said the beavers.

"Have at it," said raccoon.

"We work at night," said the beavers.

"I don't pay overtime," said raccoon.

"It's pro bono—for the good of the forest," said the beavers.

And it was a good thing they had arrived with their improvements because a bear and her cubs were the next arrivals at the pool party. They made a big splash and emptied most of the water onto the grass. What a commotion ensued.

So, the beavers worked through the night felling and hauling trees. By morning, it was just a question of packing mud into the dam with their tails and then watching water from the stream that they had diverted trickle into the new pond. It was as if the Army Corps of Engineers had arrived to save the day—without heavy equipment.

"Did you pull permits?" asked raccoon.

"Shhhhh," said the beavers. "This pond has 'always been here.' No earth greater than 10 yards was moved for this project, right? And no objection from the homeowner."

Raccoon just looked the other way. "Everybody in!" he yelled, and the critters donned their swim trunks and paddled away. Now there was even room for bears on inner tubes. And a diving board.

Today, circling high up above, I noticed some bald eagles. I worried that they were going to dive on the ducklings swimming oblivious circles in the shallow end.

"Nah. I brought them in to keep the seagulls away," said the raccoon. Wile E. Raccoon, that is. He was hiring. "The time has come for a second lifeguard," he explained, through his new diving mask and snorkel.

And then the porcupines waddled in and my imaginary pond life emptied out fast.

My Vorpal Blades: My Life in Knives

Knives were an early fascination, a rite of passage. I can measure my life in knife phases. It's your first tool—heck, the first tool of our species—and I never leave home without one. Call it an enchantment with a life-long pocket object.

I have Mom to thank. Her L.L. Bean sheath knife with the leather handle which I admired and coveted, was the emblem of my woodsman aspirations. Sure, Dad had knives too, but they were little pocketknives—utilitarian, with files and scissors—not destined for the campfire, whittling, and making backcountry camps. Dad's pocketknife would be little use fileting the trout I intended to catch or making Paleolithic torches and shelters.

When would I be old enough to have a knife of my own? Access to knives can be fraught, for parent and child. When to allow? What kind? What to keep secret from Mom and Dad? How to surreptitiously acquire and then hide them? Among my own brood, I have chosen to make knives a requirement. They make terrific graduation and birthday presents.

"Dad, I'm going out," my daughters say.

"Got your knife?"

"*Dad . . .*"

And yet how often have they seen me solve a problem by whipping out my jackknife to slice, slit, pare, portion, or harvest . . . lupines from the front field?

In third grade, I took matters into my own hands. My new best friend in my new neighborhood had a Boy Scout jackknife he was willing to trade. It was a new market for me. I had no concept of local exchange rates. But Jeff seemed to like the crystals from the hall chandelier in our new house and we brokered a deal. Now I had a knife of my own. Soon, I traded up for a camping knife complete with fold-out spoon and fork and sundry other blades; saw, file, clippers, and pick. I could MacGyver anything—and MacGyver had yet to be created! Mom never noticed the missing crystals.

Soon thereafter, Mom allowed me my dream knife: an L.L. Bean camping knife with leather sheath even longer than hers! I still have it. It may only serve as a letter opener today, but for many years it accompanied me on all my backcountry camping trips for campfire cooking. It was superb for making spears and spruce gum torches too. And when I cut myself I chalked up the injury to experience and made sure Mom never found out. This, children, is paleo-raising of one's parents. I have no idea if my own kids have spared me the gory details. That's as it should be.

In tenth grade, a friend presented me with a stiletto he had acquired in Spain. Very cool. The acme of *knife*. It was my lark, carrying it around London in my pocket, like a secret foil of danger. But a problem arose when it was time to move back to the States. I taped it securely to the lid of my drum equipment box—a heavy load of metal stands and hardware—and it was loaded into the container being shipped home. When the contents arrived, my equipment box was singled out, my parents said, by the customs official observing the delivery. The box had a padlock on it. I had conveniently "lost" the key. It could not be opened. Omérta. A teenager with a stiletto did not squeal on himself. The stiletto remained in my possession and went off to college with me where I traded it to a roommate. I had outgrown its *frisson*.

Now what would I do when my son arrived at the stage of being equally smitten with knife-as-emblem? Spencer had a hankering for his own sheathed knife. Who was I to argue. I took him to a local flea market to search for a suitable blade. We scoped out the possibilities from the vendors spreading their wares on plywood tables. A very long blade—think Bowie knife—jumped out at him. Spencer plunked his savings down without negotiation and trotted off with his prize.

I'm less armed and dangerous nowadays, though there's always a knife in my pocket. Today it's a Laguiole, the classic French shepherd's knife. Oh, to be on a hillside in Béarn carving a baguette and local cheese. Ever my emblem, now a mnemonic for thinking about scenes I'd like to inhabit, the knife at least inspires an imaginary menu and location. I may use it mostly for opening shipping boxes from Amazon, or slicing apples at lunch; opening the mail. Seems like a good chef's knife is my new longing. Or a paring knife. Nothing like a good crisp julienne slice, or apple coring for breakfast. The definition of utilitarian shifts. Even Spencer would drop big bucks on the right knife for preparing his short ribs or slicing tuna for sushi. And I'd drop big bucks on a good bread knife—still, my emblem.

Ox Cart Man

In October of the year,
he counts potatoes dug from the brown field,
counting the seed, counting
the cellar's portion out,
and bags the rest on the cart's floor.

WE AMERICANS ARE TYPICALLY only a couple of generations away from a family farm. I'm reminded of it every time I read a certain poem by Donald Hall, and every time the school bus routes and back-to-school sales are published in the press for the new school year. It's one of the last vestiges of our agrarian past: the school calendar.

I no longer have the August teacher dreams I once did, but there's still a pang when that calendar no longer applies to me. Just when the foliage dies back in the potato field, the harvest awaits digging and collection in the soil, I am an observer of the cherished rhythm of planting, harvesting, and marketing like the farmer in the poem.

The opening days of school and reading "Ox Cart Man" go together for me in theme and teaching practice. How often I used to read and reread this poem in October of the year—with my new English classes, with fellow teachers, with myself—as the new school year unfolded. In the poem's agrarian ritual, the

farmer walks to Portsmouth to sell a year's worth of crops—
"potatoes, and the bag that carried potatoes, flaxseed, birch
brooms, maple sugar, goose feathers, yarn"—then cart, then ox,
before walking home to his farm. For me, it's just like the ritual
of the school year.

By the time you get to October, the fresh rhythm has been
established and you feel like the oxen are pulling the cart. It's a
familiar road, at an unfamiliar pace; or vice versa. The new class
of students has grown into their back-to-school sneakers and
pants; the new backpacks are a little scuffed and lackluster; the
new seating arrangement is comfortable; an ease and satisfying
commerce begins. One hopes. We are on our way to the fair to
sell our "potatoes, brooms, sugar, and yarn."

Schools harvest in June; now is sowing time—yes, a reversal
of the spring planting and fall harvesting cycle. Schools too are
building on the enrichment of last year's crop and preparing to
load the wagon heading for June, with the new potatoes and
feathers of learning. And every year it is a new wagon, new seed;
new varieties. Some gets saved for the farm itself and some is
spent on supplies and, presumably, the taxes and materials that
support this "farm." The learning reseeds itself.

The family too. My granddaughter has entered preschool, the
first of the next generation to enter our family business. Freya is
in the Butterfly Room. Mango, her furry sloth pal, tags along
too, suspended from her backpack. Today there will be circle
time and nap time and colors and letters and numbers and playground. And snack. She is 14 blocks high and learning to sit at
a table for drawing with her parallel pals. She parts her hair in
the middle with two pigtails and knows the names of her family members. I am Opa. Morning hairdos are a new thing and
getting up early and into the car. And she has a real cart: a baby
buggy, she has discovered, to push around with her cohort.

Just like her mother did a generation ago, at the schoolhouse door for her preschool years. Now she has her own class of kindergartners assembled on the rug for morning meeting, reviewing the weather, the alphabet, the schedule, the rules of recess and the early lessons of gentleness and civility. One by one she makes a connection with each child. The new mother in her joins the teacher, much as it did for me when she was still a new daughter; when fathering was still new for me; when grandfathering was still new for my father.

We romanticize farming. It's hard work, every day. Same for teaching, at every level. But the crops—oh the pleasure we get when a field of potatoes flowers; when the vegetables are vine-ripe; when the youngest child grows like a weed and marches proudly down the furrow dripping seeds for pumpkins or zinnias or friendships and playmates. If we can step back from the minutiae, the daily chores and cares of weather and seasonal volume of work; the mere multiplication tables; the occasional failures; it's the romance of growing that carries us on, that helps us to renew our labors, like Hall's farmer, who,

> *at home by fire's light in November cold*
> *stitches new harness*
> *for next year's ox in the barn,*
> *and carves the yoke, and saws planks*
> *building the cart again.*

And off to market we go, with another crop. Next year, we'll rotate the north forty. What if we planted sweet peas instead of onions? Imagine the blooms! And the soil will thank us, sequestering carbon and love and enriching the whole valley when we go to market. For our family's business is your family's business too. What are you carrying in your cart this season?

On Seeing

"MYSTERIOUS AND LITTLE-KNOWN ORGANISMS live within reach of where you sit," says Harvard biologist E.O. Wilson. "Splendor awaits in minute proportions."

Here's an invitation to observe our surroundings with fresh eyes—a second look at what shares our space. And just imagine what awaits if you abandon your comfy chair and head outdoors to inquire, explore the real, rather than virtual, world. One is experience, the other just information.

Wilsonian observation occurs in any visit to an old stump, a stand of birches, a walk through a meadow, the inspection of a giant rain puddle, an unstructured ramble through "Wiggly Woods."[1] Perhaps the elusive and shy bobcat cubs would provide an escort . . . and reward for observation. It's all about the attitude of the explorer.

Such venturing forth incubates splendid recollections like this one by Robin Wall Kimmerer in *Gathering Moss*, who reaches back into her memory and retrieves the day her kindergarten teacher, with magnifying glass, opened a whole new perspective and way of seeing the natural world—the first glimpse of the microscopic level of structure, color, and mysterious beauty. Perhaps you too have such a clear recollection—your discovery of science—all the way back in kindergarten? Perhaps you too had a teacher whose deft touch turned you into a scientist, naturalist, or artist?

"Magnified tenfold, the complexity and detail of a single snowflake took me completely by surprise," she writes. "How could something as small and ordinary as snow be so perfectly beautiful? I couldn't stop looking."

The world changed. It enlarged. Now every snowflake, drift, embankment, or snowball had new potential and definition.

What else might be awaiting discovery at this micro-level of seeing? Kimmerer talks about mosses as snowflake-like structures with a unique story to tell, just like much of the flora that kids see and learn about on any forest excursion. She remembers her teacher's revelation with lens and snowflake as "an awakening, the beginning of seeing . . . the time when I first had an inkling that the already gorgeous world becomes even more beautiful the closer you look."

It happens every year when that inaugural snowflake drifts to earth and rekindles wonder for all but the jaded. We all have childhood wonder renewed by the first snowflakes of the season.

Seeing the natural world in minute detail leads to seeing everything and anything in fresh focus, once you train your eyes. Once you've seen something through a new lens, you can't stop looking. It leads to a deeper kind of knowing. Sometimes—not often enough—we call that learning, from brook to meadow to cove; from edible plants to vernal pools; from maps and journals to island explorations.

It also exists within reach of where you now sit. Splendor, in grand or minute proportions, awaits our arrival—our fresh perception. And there are four more senses to engage. Sometimes it is the child, or biologist that sounds the alert. In my experience, it is also the poet. As e.e. cummings wrote,

now the ears of my ears awake and
now the eyes of my eyes are opened.

Such vision might help you see "the world in a grain of sand," as another splendid poet wrote, in a book within reach of where I sit.

NOTE

1. The Castine kid name for Witherle Woods.

Once More to the Stream

ONE JULY, I TOOK MY 14-YEAR-OLD SON to the wilderness stream in Maine that I had not seen since, 20 years earlier, I was a camp counselor leading a group of 14-year-old boys on a canoe trip. That trip ended with a tedious drag of canoes up the rain-swollen stream to our pick-up point. It was a journey fraught with a harrowing, near disastrous fording of the torrent to land canoes, supplies, and campers safely on the side of the river nearest the road. It was a journey that made for good storytelling, once we had lived through some anxious moments.

This summer's journey began on the saltwater coast and headed inland. We drove a hundred miles of arcanely marked backcountry roads maintained by logging companies, passing vast marshy heaths created by beavers, idyllic remote lakes, secluded hunting shacks and paper company camps. The woods were lovely, dark, and deep: Moose, bear, eagle country. As we moved further into the forest, farther from paved road and traffic, our trip took on the sense of journey away from comfortable, known realms and toward the challenge of unfamiliar paths and feelings. In this return to an old haunt of mine, we would both encounter new territory.

The stream-side campsite and its vestigial stone fire circle was identifiable after 20 years, as were a few tidy fishing camps stashed at varying intervals along the eastern shore. The state had taken protective custody of the western shore when developers threatened. The general store at the road head hadn't changed in 50 years, said the proprietor, though I didn't remember the beginner fly casting kits, Orvis felt-sole wading shoes, nor Maine State Lottery tickets. We eschewed the equipment; high top sneakers will always be my boulder stream wading footwear of choice.

Ever since third grade, when we moved from Illinois to Massachusetts, to a house near a big woods, I have enjoyed a fascination with fishing, woodsmen knives, building fires: the skills of the woods. One of my early books was *Wildwood Wisdom* by Ellsworth Jaeger, which had beautiful diagrams depicting the correct way to pitch a teepee, pack a mule, lash your bedroll to your pack board, and make sassafras tea. It conveyed the lore of a complete backwoods life. While my peers played basketball on their driveways after school, I headed for the pond in the big woods to catch frogs, make pine-tar torches, erect lean-tos and play Natty Bumpo.

And I am still just as enthusiastic about living close to the elements. As camp counselor, I was obliged to be the element of control and safety; as parent, I felt obliged to be initiator and frontiersman. What I wanted most was to be pure partner and equal participant in this hunter-gatherer induction ritual upon which I had unconsciously embarked. I wanted to go walkabout with my son.

When he was 12, Spencer spent three weeks at a wilderness camp. The boys lived in tents, built a cedar-and-canvas canoe, hiked and paddled in the mountains and rivers of the state whose license plate reads: A Natural Treasure. He experienced the landscape of my camper years; of my college summers lead-ing trips; of the summer I married and took his mother home to a canvas tent in Maine; of the wilderness stream we now stood beside.

He was ambivalent about the experience at best. Though he would not return for a second summer, to this day he loves to regale us with the hardships of camp: the miserable food, hummingbird-sized mosquitoes, cruel counselors, rancid jokes. It fails to shock. He is describing days I long for, my idylls. He has earned and enjoys his story-telling rights but declined the opportunity to collect more stories. So, I stand at the stream hoping to re-enact experience; he stands worried of the implica-tion of camping and fishing with his gung-ho father. We both wrestle with the fact that I am the camp counselor again, the Maine guide. He is my reluctant camper. How will we explore the two worlds embodied in this stream?

The moment felt like the grooves of memory and gravelly road evoked by E.B. White returning to fresh water from salt water, revisiting childhood haunts in the company of his young boy, watching the son who used to be himself as the father who used to be his father. His essay[1] has been a favorite September reading assignment in my English teaching classroom, good for linking the start of school to the transitions between seasons of life as well as affording the opportunity to imitate the timbre of White's voice.

While my father disliked fishing and was a reluctant camper, he patiently accompanied me on several expeditions. Two were epigrammatic: a creek in New York, my first fishing experience, and backpacking overnight in New Hampshire. They launched a lifelong love of the woods. Once we had dug the worms, pur-chased a new, working reel, arrived at the creek and worked out how to cast, Dad struck up a conversation with an out of work steelworker fishing the same bank. I unsuccessfully plied the flat water while turtles lazed on the sunny logs and remember the day as much for learning how to skip shale across the water. When he took us backpacking in the White Mountains, Dad spent the second day attempting to overcome the dire effects of campfire cooking. Unaffected, my brother and I picked blueberries and raspberries quite contentedly and carved our names in the log wall of the shelter. But both episodes yielded good stories.

At the stream, my son put on his waterproof waders and entered the brisk water while I ventured forth in my high tops and shorts. The sun was strong, the current powerful. Spencer caught the first fish, a small bass, which he reeled in quickly as I took pictures. He quickly caught another, while my dry flies were being ignored as I probed the riffles upstream from the pool he was working. The loveliness of the scene struck me. We were appreciating this moment together. He was not my camper; I didn't have to lead him into the experience. He had his own reasons for enjoying what we shared. Hearing Spencer tell the story of fishing weeks later made me realize that it is the lore, the storytelling that we are after and that connects us. Doing it and saying it is the full experience of having it.

We caught six bass, fish we found lurking mideddy, rising to both dry flies and metal spoons. All the effort of wading the current, soaking my camera, and braving moose flies was rewarded in an instant of splendor: a modest small mouth bass hit my line just as an Osprey perched aloft a tall spruce tree, surveying the scene, unfurled his wings and took flight. I had borrowed his fish. I made sure to give it back.

We camped on the edge of a big lake, setting up our tent at dusk, cooking dinner over a fire, listening to a pair of loons call across the cove at sunset. We chopped wood, carried water;

played with matches and whittled with our knives; hid from flies. Ah, hunter-gatherer rituals. The effect was marred when our campground neighbors, sitting in their trailers, surrounded by a school of four-wheel-drive all-terrain vehicles, started their portable generators to power lights and appliances. Not everyone comes to the woods to be Natty Bumpo.

NOTE

1. "Once More to the Lake," E.B. White.

A Paean to a Blueberry Season Foretold

KERPLINK, KERPLANK, KERPLUNK. You know what I'm talking about.

This is a summer sound. It will be heard on a windy, sunny day here in Robert McCloskey country. One morning I will think, *Atop our favorite blueberry picking hill the berries are finally pickable.*

We will have come to gather food for the winter, like the bears. These berries will fuel our hibernation. We dream all winter of such a day on these barrens—every time we go to the freezer to deplete our stash of summer blueberries.

Our blueberries will end up in muffins, pies, scones, and buttermilk pancakes. In fact, once our picking trips start it will be weeks before we eat a meal that does *not* include blueberries in some form. The berry density of muffins must not fall below 25 per cubic inch.

These are not cultivated blueberries, flavorless and as big as marbles; the ones we've grown accustomed to in the supermarkets for months. These berries are tiny, wild, the *essence* of blueberry. And essence includes labor at the source for the tasty payoff. We are picking at the primal farm. The fruit grows here because it belongs here on the rocky barrens, and always has.

It takes a long time to earn a mouthful. It's not like picking strawberries—a couple of stoops, a few handfuls, and you've got two quarts and can head home. Just one quart of wild blueberries will take you thirty minutes to pick; more likely an hour, since the amount going into the pail will pale in comparison with the amount going into your mouth. *Kerplink.*

"One for me, one for you, two for me, one for you," I say to my pail. *Kerplunk.*

On one such day, our daughter, Ariel, said, "I hope some momma bear doesn't mistake me for her cub." She has read *Blueberries for Sal* enough times to know that people and bears must share their wild blueberry patches, and if their paths should overlap someone must courteously yield to the creature with prior claim, or bigger paws. Today we are the only critters in the patch.

Walking to the car, we top off our tummies with a few more handfuls of berries from our buckets. So many left to harvest! So hard to make it all the way home without consuming the whole morning's work!

However, we will pass the homemade ice cream stand at the head of the bay. They do make an awfully good chocolate chip ice cream cone. I must admit: man does not live by blueberries alone.

Whatever the berries, may your summer berry patch be wild and abundant. May the bears share generously with you. . . . and you with them.

Kerplunk.

The Christmas Table

IN ELEVENTH GRADE SHOP CLASS, I worked all fall making a dining room table. It would be a Christmas present for my parents. My teacher suggested the project based on something he had seen in a woodworking design book—a butcher-block table five feet in diameter. It was the biggest shop project I had ever done.

Week after week, during the two periods before history class, I worked away, sawing two-inch-thick pine boards into square strips, laminating them into 12-inch sections, joining the sections, and then cutting a circle out of the large square blank. After weeks sanding the round top, I had a heavy, smooth wafer. Coat after coat of oil and finish were applied. I buffed it to a golden luster. Then I built a solid base. It was not quite a Shaker reproduction, but it was constructed with similar affection. "Hands to work, hearts to God," as they said. Done.

Almost. It weighed half a ton. My plan was to move it by car under cover of darkness and sneak it into the house on Christmas Eve. Though I did not yet have my driver's license when I began the project, I scheduled my road test at the registry of motor vehicles just a week before Christmas. I had one shot at getting my license in time for my delivery date. I did. Plan B would have risked arrest.

After school one day, I moved the table to a friend's barn as my staging area, and at midnight on Christmas Eve I wrapped it in blankets and strapped it to the roof of our old Volvo station wagon, drove it across town, and eased up our driveway, headlights off. With great stealth, my brother and I rolled it through the front door and into the dining room, set it on its pedestal base, and covered it with a sheet.

In the morning, I unveiled it. Mom cried. Dad was impressed. My pleasure in making it and giving it away was far greater than any pleasure I remember from receiving gifts—that year, or any year. We ate Christmas dinner on my table.

As I look back it feels as if I was setting the table for so much more. Many years later, the table came to my own house where, by then, a series of infants had joined the dinnertime conversation. Five new Nelsons, in a new family that I couldn't have imagined in eleventh grade, spent many a meal laughing and talking and spilling juice before that table was finally relieved of duty and sent to Table Valhalla.

These memories returned when I read Matthew Crawford's *Shop Class as Soul Craft* recently. "Shared memories attach to the material souvenirs of our lives," writes Crawford, "and producing them is a kind of communion, with others and with the future."

He built his own mahogany table at a time when he "had no immediate prospect of becoming a father, yet . . . imagined a child who would form indelible impressions of this table and know that it was his father's work."

I like a table as a metaphor for all the ways in which we gather ourselves together. Aren't we always setting the table and inviting one another to dine, in one sense or another? A class, a school, a home, a community—we gather at the table of learning, friendship, sustainability, mirth, ritual, civility, and spilling juice. If we can see ourselves as sharing a table, we can see one another in a very accurate and true sense. We can share. We can pass the bread.

Most teachers would recognize the feelings of table maker and host, fashioning sturdy lives that they cannot quite predict out of vocabulary lessons and the multiplication tables. We share a few "meals" and move on to the next sitting, to take place in myriad places and times of evolving lives. Our children will, we hope, think back on the shop projects we've shared, a multigenerational gathering of makers and hosts.

"I imagined the table fading into the background of a future life," says Crawford, "the defects in its execution as well as inevitable stains and scars becoming a surface texture enough that memory and sentiment might cling to it, in unnoticed accretions."

We abandon our shiny shop work to the wear and tear of experience, children, and life, allowing it to acquire the burnishing and patina of use and rugged care. My big round table had countless lovely scratches, burns, and dings that made it all the more precious.

Today, we gather around an old architectural drafting board-turned-dining-table. It came from my wife's father, Lowell Brody, and bears the pinholes, grooves, and scribbles of his early draftsmanship, back when architects used pencils, rulers, and slide rules instead of computer-assisted design programs. "Move door to left," or "Window goes here," can still be discerned in the impressions that he routed in the wood, vestiges of clients and projects lost to memory but preserved beneath the blueprint by the pressure of sharp lead bearing down to write instructions for the builder.

And now children and grandchildren and even a great grandchild that the young architect couldn't have imagined sit and re-imagine him, working back in time thanks to the "stains and scars" on a humble few planks of dark, storied wood.

Far and Away

NOWADAYS, IT SEEMS IMPOSSIBLE TO GET AWAY. Distance is no longer romantic and exhilarating as it once was. As far as you go, as remote as you may seem, as far up the wild valley trail as you can hike, as far off the beaten path as you can wander, you're still immediately, electronically available.

When I was a lad, adventure started just out of range of a parent's voice—to be down the street, deep in the woods, paddling a boat, biking across town, digging in the back yard, or even going briefly on a walkabout. "Come back by dinner," was the only guardrail. Mom never asked where I was going; what I was doing. What, if anything, did she know? What did she not need to know?

"Where did you go?"

"Out."

"What did you do?"

"Nothing."

Sound familiar? The parental tether lengthened, stretched, and eventually broke, as it's intended to. Or was it the 'rents letting go? Either way there was a benign, grit-encouraging, and healthy disconnect.

"Away" was the forest log redoubt built by the neighborhood gang. It was a tent 15 miles up the trail from where you'd been dropped off three days ago. It's deciphering a foreign accent or ordering lunch in a language you barely speak. It's unfamiliar smells, sounds, and footsteps on paving stones. It's a left-hand drive car, winter without snow, beaches with sand. It's best served "far."

Communication used to reinforce distance, like my college year far and away. Airmail from Scotland to Illinois was the only medium for keeping in touch—paper, postage, time spent composing, followed by days awaiting an out of synch response, my fiancée and I always five days behind. Now the Internet spans time and distance—for free. And yet, there's a phantom cost—the loss of feeling far away.

What would it be like to resume paper, envelopes, and postage? My friend, Pierre, just got a typewriter. As a known typewriter aficionado, I was his first letter recipient. He regaled me with the purchase of his "Contessa," discovered languishing in a second-hand shop in Poullaouen, France.

"She's orange, from the 1960s, used, but perfect. It's noisy—more like music. A stirring music. I think it's a good way to disconnect from smartphone and computer," he typed. "One task at a time: typing. Nothing disturbing you (email, notifications, messages. . . .). I am focused on my ideas and my fingers, like a writer at the first page of a new novel." Call me Pierre.

We are between letters; far and away from one another—and this is more satisfying than an almost real-time email exchange.

But then, this morning, my daughter was strolling my old neighborhood in London. My smartphone rang. We strolled together, using FaceTime, down the familiar streets, the "muttering retreats" of my 14- to 16-year-old self. How many layers of the meaning of "distance" inhabited that experience—temporal, geographic, generational, psychological?

She passed the Builders Arms, our corner pub; then the blue plaque on T.S. Eliot's red brick apartment building and approached the entrance to mine. I imagined the elevator doors parting to take me home to the sixth floor after school; or back from an evening exploring the great city. How can I be simultaneously 16 and have a young adult daughter abroad and having this digital rendezvous "in" London? *This is far and away inhabiting a time warp*, I thought—1970/London in my pocket.

Then a friend sailing the Caribbean, having detected our impending Nor'easter, sends his regards, and a photo of tropical waters, sunshine, iguanas, and warm trade winds. On Exuma, the sand is like sugar; the water azure. He is far, but not away, and watching weather systems only his northern friends will be obliged to worry about. I'll have what he's having? Nah. Let it snow.

Then Jean also enquires about temperatures and snowfall. "J'ai vu à la télé que l'est de Etats Unis est sous la neige," Jean emails. "If you have any "belles" photos, I'll put them on our Facebook." Photos are sent—snow clinging to the trees, from the same device receiving his email—and appear instantaneously on Facebook "in" France. The world is now flattened. In fact, the point seems to be to maintain attention and connectivity at all costs; sending and receiving 24-7 in simultaneity.

Sure, I want to find "away" again. Is it still there? Can you even get there from here? Everything's all here and now, like contentment. But who wants contentment when we're continuously glimmered by the shiny objects of more and better and prettier—the bargain we make with our devices to always stay in constant touch and be kept in touch with everyone else. Tethered again—this time to our own desires and curiosities.

"Where did you go?"

"Out."

"I know."

"What did you do?"

"Nothing."

"I know."

"Would you like a new bathing suit, sun hat, herbal supplements, or sandals from our catalog?"

"No. Siri, go away!"

I hate being followed.

Reaching the
Outer Buoy
of Summer

JOHN KEATS NEVER RAMBLED on Mount Wallamatogus in Penobscot, Maine, the mound of scuffed granite that slopes down to the Northern Bay of the Bagaduce River. But had he been with Lesley and me yesterday it would have inspired an ode to Autumn.

Surely we were wandering in the romantic poet's "season of mists and mellow fruitfulness" as we climbed through blueberry barrens to the summit cairn and a clear view all the way south to Isle au Haut, as mists snuggled the inlets and valleys.

We were moved to walk the hill when the wind off the bay contained a whiff of brisk change. The timing between summer and autumn here can catch you off-guard. The maple leaves are not yet turning, the acorns are still plumping on the branch, but there is a palpable tipping point and the onset of a new autumnal rhythm. Were we there yet?

We are in no hurry to be mounting the studded snow tires or caulking the sashes. There is a certain kind of day, however, when you sense that you've reached the seasonal outer buoy. The next tack had better be down the reach, under a small jib, toward home and snug harbor.

As we gazed at the land below us, it was hard to tell which season we were tipping toward. The farmers had cut and baled their hay and tucked it in the barns. Our own meadow clamored tipping point of chores. A final pass with the brush hog? Or, let it go? It won't grow much longer. And is the woodpile sufficient for a whole winter's heat?

On 'Togus, we expected to find that the blueberries had been all picked or were starting to dry into wild "raisins" on the sun-drenched bushes. But the hill surprised us with "mellow fruit-fulness." No surprise to Keats. Autumn, he found, contained a second harvest and plentiful blossoming to the discerning eye, not just a *segue* to winter or the shutdown of summer.

As we emerged from the woods onto the barrens, we were greeted by that unlikely empurpled hillside. Some berries showed a slight puckering, but for the most part, the low, wild bushes were heavy with big, plump berries—New Jersey-size berries, but with wild Maine flavor; sweet handfuls as our fingers combed the twiggy branches. Autumn, Keats says, is for glean-ers. We meandered the hillside, picking the sweetest midnight-blue fruit from around the granite outcroppings. We grazed like bears storing up for the winter.

Keats was a gleaner, too—not so much of what was actually there, as what he *felt* about what was there. Keats gleaned poems from his own ripeness for inspiration, growth, and beauty. His autumn of bounty was as much an interior season as it was the mellowing of the English countryside.

Poets are society's gleaners, scooping up thoughtful morsels left in the furrow after the haste of prosaic harvesters. You need to walk slowly and look carefully to see fruit in unexpected places.

I began to detect a few lingering feelings of the season just past. I wanted to be a gleaner of summer, not autumn. I hadn't fully appreciated the thoughts and rhythms of summer. That outer buoy was marking a further channel to navigate. I opened communications with myself and sailed into romantic waters.

Pausing got my attention. There are too many choppy currents that throng what we allow for slack time—a propulsion to be going, doing, making—as if outward industry is all that counts as achievement. Because it is the season to pause, summer confronts us with the interstices of life. Time elongates, allowing us to see pockets of thought that were blurred as we passed by at a brisk trot.

Sometimes it's good to miss the forest for the trees. Gazing too far in the distance makes us steer as the crow flies. Picking out unique artifacts in the foreground stimulates meandering, and we savor the subtle textures of our progress: the perfume of spruce, the grasshoppers in the tomato plants, the crows caucusing on the knoll.

Keats would approve of my hammock. "Mowing can wait," he would say. Tomorrow morning we will make muffins with those blueberries. Soon enough we will make time for apple picking. But in a hammock this late summer/early autumn evening, Keats and I are listening to "gathering swallows twitter in the skies." Maine is a transcendental state of mind.

The Knowledge
Redux

When I was in high school, we lived in London for two years because my father was a journalist. He loved to talk with London cabbies, when we rode in taxis, and they always happily reciprocated. Dad particularly admired what they called, simply, The Knowledge, their encyclopedic, analog, surficial understanding of London streets, from A to Z, forward and backward, inside and out.

As preparation for their licensure, the apprentice cabbies exhaustively canvassed the metropolis on mopeds, studying maps and driving every road, place, mews, embankment, walk, court, lane, palace gate and high street, and the myriad parks, gardens, ovals, squares, rows, and closes for which London is famous. They were preparing for The Test on The Knowledge, and a unique kind of knowledge it was. Their prodigious knowledge of routes and locations is on the wane, I fear, for we no longer need to carry any knowledge around with us—there's always an app for that.

Everyone's a cabbie these days, alas, pitted against Uber, Lyft, and the GPS navigation that's on everyone's phone. But we are all being pitted against a world based increasingly on information and not experience. We *are* the cabbie, knowing the texture of our city, the granular detail and how it has changed over time; who lives here and there and how a neighborhood or village is evolving. Google Maps only knows the cold, hard data of the street number and name, though every so often the Google photo van captures a human moment as it drives by and scans the high street. It has a humanizing effect. I have a friend who was photographed peering over the garden wall of his own house, in France, as the Google truck surveyed his domain.

I took my first Lyft ride last May in San Francisco. It was great. The driver and I got acquainted on the drive from the airport into the city center—just like a real cabbie conversation. But Lyft and Uber are not taxis, in the old London cabbie sense. The Lyft driver simply owns the car and the coordinate-locating device, not The Knowledge. Theirs is an app-intensive experience, from start to finish, driver and passenger included. You "hail" the "cab" using an app on your smartphone. Pretty slick. I'm not complaining, just making an observation about two different kinds of experience. The Lyft driver responds to coordinates and will be driving down streets never before experienced. It's a comparison that stands for so much more than getting from one place to another by navigating surface arteries.

I am a bit of a curmudgeon in this respect. Ours has become a digital-versus-analog world; an information-versus-experience interface; coordinates versus directions; data versus narrative. The digital watch tells you what time it *is*. The good old analog watch face contains time past, present, and future.

Consider how you give directions. "Take Route 1 north to Bucksport, then east to Route 15. Follow that south to Blue Hill." It'll work.

Or, "Take the Acadia Highway to the Penobscot Narrows Bridge by Fort Knox. Cross to Bucksport and follow the signs to Bar Harbor and Acadia. Then, at the Big Apple, take the Front Ridge Road South, past the Blueberry Freezer, Horse Power Farm, The Halcyon Grange, and into the village of Blue Hill at the top of Blue Hill Bay." Enjoying the ride a little more, given some scenic views?

I once had to rendezvous with a friend on a backroad. "See you at the chicken barn," he said. The structure is no longer there, but it remains a point of reference. Mission accomplished, among locals. And I bet there are plenty of other people who could still meet me there. No Uber need apply. Directions have a story. Coordinates only have location. The younger generation eschews the wristwatch as a single-purpose device. I eschew the schizophrenia of its latter-day replacement: myriad apps, music, news, time, and temperature all on a pocket universe of telecommunications tied to a cloud.

Not so fast. Google may be the apotheosis of mapmaking: digitized coordinates that combine with visual narrative and create an uncanny remote experience. When the eye in the sky of its satellite view combines with Google's little orange man-icon dropping to the street, it can be an astounding altered reality. I know it's possible, for instance, to take the street address of your great great grandfather's home from the 1850 Census in Scotland, insert it in the satellite view window, and descend from the clouds to Wester Broom Cottage. It's on the main road in the village of Spott, just west of Dunbar, on the east coast of Scotland. I can "stand" before the actual wee stone cottage in which Alexander Nelson lived with his parents James and Agnes and six siblings. Although there are now cars parked out front where there would formerly have been a horse cart and farm road, it is the very same structure from 1850. The fields his father plowed are just behind the house, and still being farmed. I guess that's generated a pretty special humbling kind of knowledge, for me. But it's still the experience that I bring to that photo that makes the connection, for it was I who knew and chose where to look.

Going Through the Stones[1]

I AM IN INVERNESS. It is October 1970. My ninth grade class has taken the overnight train from London for a long weekend of tourism around the capital of the highlands: Loch Ness, Castle Urquhart, and the monastery on the shore of the loch where Nessie once appeared to a monk. We stay at the Caledonian Hotel, in the heart of town, on the River Ness connecting Moray Firth and the North Sea with Loch Ness. We get little sleep.

I am in Inverness. It is June 1971, and three dozen Outward Bound students have piled into the back of a lorry for a cold, bumpy ride from Moray Sea School in Burghead to the battlefield at Culloden, where the Jacobites met disaster (slaughter) at the hands of the English in 1745. Now we're having a walkabout in the "big city."

I am in Inverness. It is a cold and dreary February day in 1977, and Ian McFadyen and I have been circuiting the Western Highlands in his VW beetle. Ian is a wee man, perhaps 5'2". I am over 6'. Folding myself to sleep in the front seat of the VW, for a third night, is just not gonna happen. Last night, somewhere in the Western Highlands, I had to open the door and roll onto the pavement of the forlorn layby, to stretch out in my sleeping bag. Anything to unbend. I awoke with grazing sheep staring at me. Tonight we have a room in the MacDonald House Hotel and sleep well. Full Scottish breakfast awaits, including kippers, blood pudding, grilled sausages, and porridge. It is my junior year abroad at Stirling University and Ian and I live in Murray Hall on the campus. In June, I'll be home, getting married, wearing my bespoke Gunn tartan kilt, then return to Bates College for my senior year, ready to write a senior thesis on T.S. Eliot, inspired by a Stirling seminar on Pound, Eliot, and Auden.

I am in Inverness. It is March 1981. My wife and I are staying at MacDonald House. The record of my previous visit is in the guest book. We sign again. We take the county bus out of town to Castle Urquhart on Loch Ness; visit House of Frasier highland clothing shop; then take the train back to Edinburgh. Onward to London, Lesley's birthplace; my high school home; Sassenach capitol.

I am in Inverness. It is late June 2011. We are spending the night at MacDonald House. Our daughter, Ariel, just received her BFA from Glasgow School of Art. We have driven south from Caithness after spending a week in a restored stone croft owned by friends, Simon Verity and Martha Finney. Simon is carving a memorial map to British victims of September 11 in New York's Hanover Square Garden, carved from Caithness flagstone and Moray sandstone. His carving tools and a stockpile of stones are stacked in the shed out back. When in Caithness, Simon works on secret stone carvings hidden along the shoreline, his registry for the ages. On the croft door step he has carved "haste ye back."

I've walked the headlands around John O' Groats, dotted with sheep, imagining my Viking forebears attempting to land in the scant inlets along the abrupt cliffs. Clan Gunn is still headquartered nearby. I gaze across the Pentland Firth to Orkney. Next trip. In the morning, we'll return our rental car and take the train back to Glasgow. We sign the guest registry.

I am in Inverness. It is a dreary, *dreich*, day in early September 2019. I've taken the train up from Aberdeen. The Caledonian Hotel is now the Mercure Hotel Inverness. I stroll the river side past MacDonald House. Vacancy. I visit Leakey's Second Hand Books, a two-story trove of art prints, Ordinance Survey maps, books of all sorts, and the ambience only gently worn volumes can provide. It's an old stone church. I dig out a few classic Ordinance Survey maps of places I've been, and a print of a fishing dory on the beach in Balintor, on Moray Firth. I've been there too, sailing across the firth from Burghead in Outward Bound cutters, to camp on the beach. Back in Aberdeen that evening, Ariel has just qualified for her MFA degree from Robert Gordon University. Earlier in the week, I picked up my first kilt in Edinburgh where it was remade to fit my son.

I am in Inverness. I don't know when—preferably not Jacobite times. So far, going through these stones delivers me only to the past. One of these days, perhaps, I'll have traveled forward in time. Since time seems to unfurl in only one direction, I guess I'll have to wait and see. Actually, I'm living in the future now, if past is prelude.

NOTE

1. Or, Craigh na Dun, the hilltop mystical stones near Inverness that are a portal between past and present in the *Outlander* saga. Unfortunately, they are but Styrofoam megaliths created in the studio for filming on location at Kinloch Rannoch, not Inverness.

The Word for World Is Forest

TOLKIEN KNEW; Ursula le Guin figured it out; the poets certainly know: The wisdom of the trees is more ancient and pervasive than our own. My insights have little depth compared with the oak grove—my bower—surrounding my house. The forest has been talking to itself, as itself, for 450 million years. It knows best, and it knows all. The fantasy parlance of the Ent Moot isn't quite so fantastical. As it turns out, there's scientific affirmation of exquisite tree communications. Trees are fluent in sustainability. We should listen.

There's a forest telegraphy occurring beneath our feet, I've learned, through the massive and microscopic fungal networks that translate the needs of one tree species to another; that sponsors arboreal communiqués far beyond the visible root system. It signals and antidotes disease. It runs the mutual aid society that undergirds the forest's health care system. Yes, forests are socialist, or to use a less humanly fraught term, mutualist. Though there is such a thing as tree-species dominance and competition, forests mostly know how to get along. They thrive on diversity, and the removal or failure of one species can affect societal health. So, they have a "non-hierarchical network between numerous kinds of plants."

In *Underland*, Robert MacFarlane has a way of blending the scientific and poetic parlance on this topic. Arborists and ecologists refer to the "understory," he writes, "the life that exists between the forest floor and the tree canopy. . . . Metaphorically, though, the "understory" is also the sum of the entangled, ever-growing narratives, histories, ideas and words that interweave to give a wood or forest its diverse life in culture." I would say, we are healthiest when we identify as participants in this understory—when we achieve and embrace membership, for it is certainly thrust upon us regardless.

Underground, among the hair-roots, there's a conversation going on. Trees talk, commiserate, share, protect one another. Is there more to this anthropomorphism? Can one say trees have empathy? Do they mourn? What is affection between trees? If left alone, the forests know what to do. Experiments with radioactive carbon isotopes have proven how trees redistribute resources. They nurture, mother, even recognize kin. There is wisdom in the life of trees that we've only just begun to understand—such newcomers to the notion of planetary ecology. Perhaps our survival lies in imitation of the mutuality of the trees. They show great humanity. Or, is arborpomorphism a word? Should be.

We have our own root system and verbal mycorrhizal network in poems, our verbal understory of feeling, wisdom, voices of ancestors, and companionship and interconnection that transfers resources. Poetry too is mutuality. For me, it is the meta-arboreal realm of my species, where the information stored and transmitted by our poets runs like sap from human to human, wizened sugar maple to sapling. Poetry is an isotope!

Howard Nemerov's paean to trees, for instance:

> *To stand for the constant presence of process*
> *And always to seem the same;*
> *To be steady as a rock and always trembling,*
> *Having the hard appearance of death*
> *With the soft, fluent nature of growth,*
> *One's Being deceptively armored,*
> *One's Becoming deceptively vulnerable;*

Or W.S. Merwin, mourning an old walnut tree of his acquaintance:

> *you and the seasons spoke the same language*
> *and all these years I have looked through your limbs*
> *to the river below and the roofs and the night*
> *and you were the way I saw the world*

Everyone ought to have a favorite tree. My daughter's is the lone oak in Arthur Wardwell's pasture. Mine was the ancient white pine I used to climb in my grandmother's suburban yard. Each summer I measured my strength and daring with a climb, higher and higher, in its august branches. The smell of its pitch on my hands and the drone of cicadas are deep summer memories. Now I love a copper beech, older than human settlement in my town, and the oak tree that my granddaughter will spend hours perching in and decorating—Freya's tree.

My walks in the woods are altered. I know I tread on synapses and discourse. My trees are always gossiping and commemorating: me, the farmer who was their prior "owner," their response to the clearing and harvesting and reseeding of their own domains. They respect one another's space in the canopy and embrace one another's need of root-space more than I do. I like Joseph Campbell's view: "The goal of life is to make your heartbeat match the beat of the universe, to match your nature with Nature." And Richard Wilbur says, "How much we are the woods we wander in." It's a tree view. I'd like it to be so. In my mind, it's a moot point.

A Little Leaven

OPEN ANY COOKBOOK TO THE INDEX. Embedded in the potential menu for tonight's dinner is the story of language, geography, family history, migrations, inventions, chemistry, farming, commerce, and botany. A recipe is more than the sum of its ingredients.

Take bread, the human family's most common food. Everyone eats it, and the bread you eat says a lot about who you are. Bread, I'd like to think, is why people stopped hunting and gathering to cultivate grain. (It led to beer too.) It's why we settled down. You must farm to have bread, and you need bread if you farm. It's an Ur food of the two grand human parties, nomads and settlers. Fine dining had begun, though. Coming soon: the grilled cheese sandwich; the baguette; brioche.

Bread is a Rosetta Stone of family, culture, commerce; settlement and dispersal; trading and hoarding; invention; simplicity; nourishment. Yes, it's also food: memorable, satisfying, sensuous, fragrant, fundamental. Who doesn't feel home is the place redolent of the fragrance of yeast proving; of dough rising, loaves baking; of crusty loaves coming out of the oven.

Bread tells stories. It narrates our geography, past and present locale. It resides in our cities and countries, some persisting only in the remembrance of a recipe's name. Pissaladiere, Challah, pain du nord africain au coriander, lama bi ajeen, pita, pannetone, lefse, barra brith, barm brack, bunuelos, Pain de mie, kugelhopf, verterkake, bagels, bannock, Broa, Choreki, Christopsomo, pizza caccia nanza. Every Scottish grandmother has a shortbread recipe. Rugelach is gestalt.

Is your family represented in this list? Bread came with your people from wherever your people came from, the compass round. Bread is like that. Though we may have arrived at baking in very different ways, at different times in the long memory of bread, every culture has its unique bread. "The staff of life," the breadbasket of the world, the earliest loaf in the cradle of civilization—bread has accompanied us on our human pilgrimage. Day by day the manna fell. Bread is a democratic republic.

Be it leavened or unleavened, breaking bread leavens the whole lump of the potluck. In fact, I would say that the authentic leaven *is* the potluck—the seating, sharing, tolerance, of a meal among community or family members. And we are all community members. Our hands have kneaded, waited, and baked our bread; we have concocted the family secret casserole; pies, and cakes. Then we sit for the communal meal that makes us family or community and savor it.

I love the scene in the 1980s movie *Diva* that encapsulates bread's essence—admittedly, to a French man. "The bread!" explains Gorodish to his bewildered acolyte. "The knife. . . not too thin, but not too thick. The bread...fresh, but not too fresh. It's an art. We French are envied the world over, for this. Watch. You spread it. My *satori*[1] is this: Zen in the art of buttering bread. Watch. No knife, no bread, no butter! Only a gesture . . . a movement . . . space . . . the void."

Chop wood, carry water, slice and butter bread. It's the gesture of a conductor, soothing the string section or inciting the brass—no void though—conjuring and extracting music from the silence of rests in the score, interstices of notes awaiting a harmonic chord or arpeggio. I detect a secular communion like we get from the poets.

> *But we who will eat the bread when we come in*
> *Out of the cold and dark know it is a deeper mystery*
> *That brings the bread to rise:*
> > *it is the love and faith*
> *Of large and lonely women, moving like floury clouds*
> *In farmhouse kitchens, that rounds the loaves and the lives*
> *Of those around them . . .*
> > *just as we know it is hunger—*
> *Our own and others—that gives all salt and savor to bread.*

—Thomas McGrath

My satori now proofs in a big bowl, intoxicating the whole house. It rises and bubbles, alchemy of yeast, water, flour, and salt. Hunger abounds, as does nourishment. The timer says the first batch is ready to leave the oven. It has the right hollow thump. Now the loaves must cool and crackle—some call it whistling. Don't cut it too soon, though the butter and knife and palate await. Come to the table. Waiting is part of the mystery and ritual of bread and community, hunger, love, and healing the heart. And that Zen gesture. Bon appetite.

NOTE

1. A state of intuitive illumination sought in Zen Buddhism.

Great Great Great Grandfather Rutherford and Me

I EAT DINNER WITH MY GREAT GREAT GREAT grandparents every night. Breakfast too. Were they alive today, Jesse and Mary Ann Rutherford would be 217 years old, give or take. But they seem alive to me in their 180-year-old oil portraits hanging on our dining room wall. We are in regular conversation, and their eyes seem to follow me around the room. I've known them my whole life, even before they came to reside with us 30 years ago. Our turn to host the Rutherfords.

Married in 1825, Jesse and Mary Ann spent their whole lives in Pennsylvania—Erie and Philadelphia. In their afterlife, they have toured the country, from Boston to California to Illinois to Maine to Pennsylvania and back to Maine. We never leave home without our 19th century kin: our itinerant forebears and oldest visual representation of an ancestor. Their oil portraits are probably the Sears photo studio of their day, painted by an anonymous Philadelphia portrait painter, and they look none the worse for wear as they preside over our meals.

The older I get, the more my friends detect a family resemblance between Jesse and me. Is it the nose? The hairline? The Scottish borders pallor? Not many people can visualize their 19th century family members, nor have 19th century kin following them into the future, like an *Outlander* meme. I have their DNA. Their eyes follow me in that respect too.

Before they came to my house, Jesse and Mary Ann graced the living room walls in Grandfather Stone's house. His mother was a Rutherford, Jesse and Mary Ann's granddaughter. I've delved into this family lineage seeking Jesse's origins. His father was Jacob, who came from Bolam, north of Newcastle, England, an area still full of Rutherfords. What would they have *sounded* like? What might a Rutherford family expression be that persists in me? Did they have a sense of humor?

Jesse died from apoplexy in Philadelphia, January 1862. He and Mary Ann had lived in Erie, where his will, drawn up in June of 1861, was probated the following September. "It is my wish . . . in case there is remaining any property, for [my wife] to dispose of . . . to divide the same on equal parts among our children or their heirs—and I do hereby constitute and appoint my wife Mary Ann Rutherford sole executor of this my last will and testament. In witness whereof I, Jesse S. Rutherford, the testator, have to this my will, written on one sheet of paper, set my hand and seal this nineteenth day of June A.D. one thousand eight hundred and sixty-one." Economical use of paper, and duly witnessed. Imagine his surprise to know who inherited his portrait.

They had several children, who had more children, who have had correspondence with our branch. I come from their son Thomas, who had a brother named William, who had a son named Clarance, whose daughter was Erma, whose descendants I'd like to find.

My grandmother wrote to Erma Rutherford Young in the 1970s, inquiring about her family knowledge, citing the oil portraits. Erma replied, "Guess if I went thru some of my old papers I might find something. We have great grandfather's sword, also his commission in the Navy (On Sheep's skin)." Jesse was a naval engineer at the time of the Civil War. Alas, this correspondence petered out and I have yet to locate its heirs.

How tantalizing to think of the naval sword, a commission on sheepskin, letters, and a better understanding of the family arc from Bolam to Pennsylvania. Just how and when did "we" get here, and why? Who on the Scottish borders might have some other family portraits allowing a comparison of family noses and pallor? And where did "we" hang the ancestors prior to Bolam? There's an urge to keep going back, and back, just as the Rutherfords accompany us on our journey forward.

How quickly family connectivity, artifacts, and lore can dissipate—even within living memory we lose the threads of our relations. I hope sword, sheepskin, and the family jewels, if any, haven't ended up on eBay's digital yard sale. I prefer to imagine them proudly displayed on the wall of some distant cousin—who wonders what their owner looked like. A historical reunion of artifacts and their owners would be nice—Jesse reunited with his sword. For now, he uses 19th century social media—1860s Instagram—to forward his éminence grise to family and lives he could never have imagined, but who exert their imagination on him, thanks to the inheritance of his visage.

Typing with America's Sweetheart

I HAD NO SOONER FINISHED WATCHING the *California Typewriter* story on CBS, than I knew I needed to write a letter to Tom Hanks. A fellow typewriter aficionado and grand collector, he waxes eloquent in the film about the feel of real typing on vintage typing machines. It is an homage to the style, heft, timbre, and tradition of manual typewriters—word processors with moving parts, inky ribbons, and cacophonous clatter. No silicon. It is the sound of thinking and writing, in my humble opinion—a sound I was raised on.

I fired off my letter—not an email. Though I'm afraid I did compose it on my laptop, it was duly printed and signed on paper. Not an electronic transmission.

Dear Mr. Hanks:

You had me at the black Royal behemoth in your CBS Sunday Morning piece about typewriters. I grew up with that machine, listening to my journalist father pound away after bed time. I still have that machine. It stares at me with encouragement.

I also have a small Hermés Rocket given to me by our local poet, Philip Booth. I like the provenance of that one, especially the worn spot from his right thumb on the space bar. Nothing like owning the machine your favorite poems were written on.

So, thanks for the stirring walk among the machines of real writing. I regretfully admit this letter was composed on a MacBook Pro.

I enclosed a photo of my father sitting at the Royal. And I did sign my note with a fountain pen—Dad's. This was duly credited by Hanks. That is, no doubt, another story.

To my great surprise and pleasure, Tom Hanks replied by mail within a few weeks. We are now BFFs.

"That Royal is a desktop mountain of a machine," he wrote. "It would last another thousand years, like mine will. What is the half-life of a good typewriter anyway?"

Hanks typed his note on a yellow telegram facsimile he calls a Hanx-O-Gram—"the surest and safest service to all the world." He thereby keeps another writing transmission memory alive—also personal to me. Long ago, my journalist father filed his stories via Western Union telegrams, after typing them on his portable Olivetti. That's how all reporters did it. I can recall accompanying him to the Reuters office in London, as late as 1971, to file copy, and I've seen the facsimiles of his typed dispatches on Western Union wires from Mississippi in 1963.

Anyone sent a telegram recently? Is it still a thing? Tom thinks so. But you must be a person of a certain age to even resonate a little to his conceit.

California Typewriter is also a small shop in Berkeley, California with a big mission: keeping typing on typewriters alive. It is a mecca for typing on machines—paper-stamping engines of true writing. Missing a letter, a spring, a connecting rod, a roller for your Smith Corona or Underwood or Hermés Rocket? They'll have it. They'll fix it. Get you back on the writing road.

Though, sadly, I hardly use my typewriter any more, it remains the dominant emblem of my life. Sure, using this MacBook Pro has a speed and seductive ease; an editing facility that the typewriter doesn't. But I realize that it also has an anti-draft conceit: there is only the *present* wording of my prose. I do not have successive copies that show my writing footprints, the evolution of my thought and expression. It doesn't show where I've come from on this writing road. As I look over Dad's Western Union typing, I can see that even as he finalized copy to send, he was editing. Words are crossed out; substitutions made. The prose is actively evolving up to the very last minute—and there is a record of it. For posterity: me. Like that big black Royal behemoth staring down at me from the shelf. It says, *writing takes muscles, intention, pauses, work . . . and rework.*

If there were a national typing day—and there should be—I would like to be the Grand Marshall of the parade of Royals and Underwoods and Olivettis going past on floats. I would tantalize my new BFF Hanks with the notion of riding along in the back seat of a suitably old school vehicle, just ahead of those writing machines with a hood like a 1955 Buick and diesel rumbling for the sound of writing production—the Ur sound of writing, for me. No silicon.

And I'm glad that Tom Hanks is finally getting some of the recognition he deserves. You might have thought it would be for his award-winning acting. But no, it's for service to the cause of typing machines.

Vernal Pools: A Love Story

LOVE IS IN THE AIR. The maples have completed their sugar download. Mrs. Fox trotted through our field, fresh mouse dangling from her lips, bringing take-out home for her new family of kits. *Eau de* skunk perfumed my yard last night. It is always skunk hour somewhere. The "force that through the green fuse drives the flower," is revving up and it's a force to be reckoned with. In fact, it may be the universal constant, like electromagnetic force—but not subject to decay by the weak force. As beat poets and lovers know, this soggy spring-Brigadoon is just *l'amour*. Rural romance is revving.

Suddenly the plot thickens and blooms. There are daffodils, crocuses, tulips, and baby birds. Black flies, and mosquitoes as big as hummingbirds, alas. Parties and party animals abound. Bullfrog Bolero beat box begins beating.

For the biologist, it could be the gospel chorus of *Pseudacris crucifer* pining for their native, amniotic pool wherefore to mate and lay eggs—new life and progeneration and next year's Peeperpalooza. "What's in a name?" Amphibian Tinder and wetland eHarmony are hard at work plying the customary sexy algorithm. The faster these spring frogmen sing, the better their chances to attract Ms. Right. The wood frogs sing back-up; usually-shy salamanders are feeling frisky too, making stealthy nocturnal moves. An amphibian orgy is underway. Fairy shrimp, moving even below a layer of ice, disco dance. Can Peaseblossom, Puck, and Oberon be lurking far offstage? One species's swampland is another's Studio 54. Full moon disco ball. Big night. Yasgur's aqua farm . . . "three days of peace, love, and music." But not sleep. Absolutely no one sleeps tonight.

The young humans too have scheduled pool parties. Soon Juliet and her tree frog Romeo will be testing the waters and dancing. The Capulet Prom beckons. Romeo buys a ticket, suits up in a powder blue tux; Juliet gets her frock on. We English majors know those "iambic bongos" when we hear them. Iamb what iamb. Let's boogie, Bard. Moon, croon, spoon, June—the song remains the same.

But we're such a complicated species. Consider the inner workings of infatuation and family feuds orbiting the waters of ill-fated romance in the vernal pool of Verona. Romeo himself seems a rogue when he has the audacity to show up at the Capulet party. He too is pining: for fair Rosalind. But once he sets his peepers on Juliet's he switches tunes. He'd rather make sweet music with Capulet's daughter; Rosalind who? He has been zapped by maple love sugar in his very cross-gartered capillaries. "Did my heart love till now? forswear it, sight! For I ne'er saw true beauty till this night."

Alas, human courtship does not always end as intended. It's never a sure thing even for peepers. Some pool prom-goers are, in fact, "star-crossed lovers," as it turns out. Love is an endangered species; the vernal pool a perennial candidate for environmental protection. Emotional watersheds need to be secured.

And what powerful mnemonic properties might this sonic drama play in the night air wafting up the bay for the local youths of our species? It could be nothing more than a preview of the tapping of those bongos, or as grave as learning when to ignore the girl from the rival gang, keep on trucking past her father's house, ignore the hothead cousin. Do not listen to Coach Mercutio or that humming in your loins. "I wanna know what love is," sings the wood frog through his moon roof, smelling like bait and Axe, hopped up in his bucket seat, yearning to burn rubber. All in good time, my friend. There's next year's prom, and the one after that. Boom shaka laka laka.

Another vernal poet gets the final word:

> *"sweet spring is your*
> *time is my time is our*
> *time for springtime is lovetime*
> *and viva sweet love"*

—E.E. Cummings

This play's the thing. Hear the beat? Nothing more basic than love, wherever your watershed. Ribbit.

Bird by Bird

MY DAUGHTER WAS STRUGGLING with her book report. It was an assignment requiring her to go beyond a synopsis of the plot in *April Morning* to delve beneath a mere recital of the list of characters and their actions. It was requiring her to step outside of her comfort zone with language.

A seventh grader, Hilary was in a bumpy transit from her competent summaries of the text to the sub-textual observations her teacher was training the class to do. The time had come in her growth as a reader and writer to explore the abstract sense of things, the figures in language, not just the concrete details of the story. It was a painful struggle. It seemed like an unfair subterfuge to learn that words could be about something other than what they say.

"I don't know what he means by this question," she moaned, rereading the teacher's assignment for the tenth time. "I can't interpret what happens. It just *happens*. There's no interpretation. It's about what it's about. That's all there is to it!"

I remembered well the parallel scene in my own schooling, how one night I worked long and hard to make the usual time-honored book report display by pasting a collage of magazine photos on oak tag, surrounding my dutiful prose regurgitation of the plot, to illustrate the trials and tribulations of the

characters in *The Outsiders*. Photographically, concretely, literally, the report took shape.

When Mr. Katz returned my hard work, his comment suggested that I needed to interpret the story, think about the *why*
of the story; think about the writer's motivation in telling the
story. Apparently, the story meant something other than what it
said. The writer had been saying one thing and meaning another.
It was about more than it was about. Go figure.

I remember what a thrill the subsequent moment of revelation
was when the "insides of words" were illuminated to me and
I left behind the illustrated book report (with fancy cover and
huge titles) forever. A writer has control over this stuff? A writer
isn't just recording "the way it happened?" I realized. The story
is something imagined! And I entered my Eric Sevareid imitation period and took a giant step away from passive acceptance
of the story and leap toward critical examination of the craft of
assembling words in a particular order, for a particular reason. I
became suspicious. The text was about more than the sum of its
parts. And I remember finding joy and new music in this gestalt.

As I listened to my Hilary's complaints and daubed her tears,
I thought of a poignant scene in a poem by Richard Wilbur. In
"The Writer," he is observing his daughter as she writes a story
"In her room at the prow of the house" and she struggles, like
a room-bound starling, to [beat] a smooth course for the right
window. . . clearing the sill of the world." He empathizes with
the hard work of comprehending words, working at choosing
the right ones, starting and stopping in the attempt to get them
down just right.

How many of my own writing students had I heard complaining about the "deep inner meanings" produced by sleight
of hand from the poetry and prose we studied in my courses?
"How do you know that the writer intended for those words

to be symbolic?" they griped. How do you know that's what it's about? Then, their objections bemused. Now, with my daughter asking the questions in frustration—now that my daughter was the starling trapped in the strange room of her writing assignment—the problem preoccupied me in a different way.

The teacher-writer-dad in me craved reconciliation of roles. But beyond that, I hoped for Hilary a successful transit to the love of the "second sight" of well-wrought language, the stuff of poems.

Howard Nemerov expressed it aptly in an invocation to a student:

> *The world is full of mostly invisible things,*
> *And there is no way but putting the mind's eye,*
> *Or its nose, in a book, to find them out. . . .*[1]

"Mostly invisible things"—the deep inner meanings, the subtext, the saying of one thing and meaning another—sounded like the hypothetical anti-matter of physics . . . or is it science fiction? The meanings, beauties, and truths posited by English teacher and dad, surely awaited somewhere beneath the words on her page. If these are the things the world is "mostly made of," they must outweigh so many things credited with weightier weight! What a world there is to gain by their appreciation. What a world we're missing if not putting the mind's eye to the lens. What the world is "about" is not what it says it's about! How else could there even be a concept of *gestalt*?

We're accustomed, of course, to a world that is carelessly worded. "It's about . . ." is a constant refrain, as if meaning were something obvious, declarative, visible, agreed upon. And what Hilary was encountering, of course, as we all do at some point, is the opening of the mind's eye. I don't think even she, sitting at the prow of the house, thought it was just "about" a book report in seventh grade.

NOTE

1. "To David, About His Education," *The Collected Poems of Howard Nemerov*, p. 268.

Our Daily Deer

IN THE SUMMER, Freya June and I walked down the road each morning. We'd been doing it all July and August. She is three and a half months old and rides in her stroller, rocked to sleep by the gravel under the wheels. I am slightly older, her teamster, wide awake and observant, on this daily *rendez-vous* with wildlife. The thrush still sings their dawn song. The crows start their shift soon. The forest prepares revelations.

The benefit of a daily stroll is observing the same route at the same time each day; an exercise in comparative appearances. Though "data analytics" is a term he would eschew, Thoreau would know the possibilities. Every walk has a background and foreground; the same route outbound and inbound, renewed with fresh possibility at each bend in the road. It's what leads us onward.

I always hope for a bear sighting. When the raspberries ripen across from the farmhouse we might get lucky. We mostly see familiar deer. One particular doe bashfully awaits at the same meadow entrance. She raises her head at our approach, exhales a warning huff, and bolts. Out venture two yearlings from hiding and follow her. For the rest of our stroll, I assume we are never more than 30 yards from a deer . . . and maybe a bear in the wings awaiting a cue?

If she is our daily doe, what are we to her? She is wildlife; we are—fellow creatures of habit. What assumption does she make about proximity to humans. *I see this guy every day! In the same place! With that sleeping bambina! How predictable.*

Yesterday a porcupine ambled toward an apple tree. Today we spied him sleeping high up in the crotch of an oak. A pileated woodpecker drummed on an enormous hollow pine tree—timber timpani tarantella reverberating through the woods. An osprey soared above the field. Loons called from the river. My grandmother taught me the birdsongs.

Not all nature is obvious until you've made several trips on several days and have glimpses to compare. The palette changes. We have nests and hollows to check on, and nesting birds about to fledge. It could be the operative word for the whole season as birds, deer, bear, and plants send forth offspring. Freya too will fledge by next summer. I anticipate the day when we'll pass the raspberry patch and a big furry head with small ears looks out, inspecting our passage. Until then, the same dark tree stump surprises me anew—our bear! Finally. Nope. Drat.

The road itself tells stories. I'm not above inspecting scat left prominently displayed. Daily greeting. But whose? Blueberries embedded. Coyote, fox, bear . . . baby bear? I become a connoisseur of scat. *Thank you for your considerate communications.* Step carefully. On the road's verge, we spy footprints and new paths through the meadow grass, and matted places that must be deer beds.

We pass human footprints too. The foundation of my neighbor's home addition progresses rapidly. The builders wave as we roll by. Concrete today; framing by the end of the week. House wrap, decking, window openings. We await rafters and roofing.

"Which way will the ridge beam run?" I ask today. North-South.

"Second story?"

"No."

"High ceilings?"

"Yup."

A big deck too, judging by the pressure-treated lumber. I can see it taking shape, with a panoramic view of the hayfield and river. Closed in soon. Ready for hibernation. Thoreau would approve, though it far exceeds his economical square footage at Walden Pond. Most of the nest builders we track are more frugal with their open concept plans.

"There is some of the same fitness in a man's building his own house that there is in a bird's building its own nest," Thoreau wrote. "Who knows but if men constructed their dwellings with their own hands . . . the poetic faculty would be universally developed, as birds universally sing when they are so engaged?"[1]

Vegetation continues its summer flowering and fruit, while some trees even now preview fall colors. Who can say what premature or late means, as season hands off to season? Seasons overlap, but autumn too has its harvests and bounty and Indian summer—"season of mists and mellow fruitfulness," said Keats. The wizened grandfather oak spreads his arms above his fledgling forest. Fledglings beget fledglings; acorns a forest. Someday, Freya will stroll her child down the road telling the stories of our deer and porcupines and nests and the thrush. And I am a fledgling grandfather. Freya, fawns, fledglings, grandfather.

For now, I'm just anticipating Freya's first word: bear. Please.

NOTE

1. *Walden*, p. 40, 46. Princeton University Press, 1973.

Whose Woods
These Are

MY NEWLY DISCOVERED PATH was hiding just over the boulder wall running along the west side of Merriam Street, an old farm lane. Paths were a revelation to me, in 1964, age eight, having just moved from the staid tree city grid of a Midwestern, suburban childhood. I was accustomed to riding my bike on concrete sidewalks and alleys with square corners, navigating by its chessboard coordinates from my house to school, to Tommy's house, to the playground, to the back alley—a world of right angles. Now, the sinuous forest path was my playground. And every path since then summons its memory, and the soft tom-tom of my feet on worn dirt.

I can still feel the rough trace under foot, crossing the field and entering the dark, massive, and secretive white pines. This would be my image for an Ent Moot years later when I finally read Tolkien, and even now as I consider the concept of "forest bathing" and the salutary effects of living in the embrace of trees. Surely these pines were *beings*. Grass verged on pine needles; open light shifted to somber shade and the path descended a soft track, crossed a vestigial bridge (careful of your balance—this is where Robin Hood cast Little John into the brook, we imagined), and opened onto an enormous fishing pond. Ten minutes from my backdoor, cutting through Jeff's yard, I was on the shore of adventure and a free-range childhood. It felt to me like wilderness.

I do not recall Mom or Dad ever accompanying me into the woods. I don't know if they even knew where I was going, traipsing out the dooryard. This was my terrain, my lark, my exploration, in the time of benign neglect and "be home by dark"-parenting. I was left to my paleo delights. I discovered fort building and fire. By collecting the white pine sap on the end of a stick, and with the help of stolen matches, Jeff and I had blazing torches, once setting the field alight, to our chagrin—stamped out just in time. The adults never knew. Soon I would have my first jackknife. Whittling followed. And knife-throwing competitions. Amazingly, little blood was spilt.

I do recall the first and last family hiking trip to the White Mountains. Somewhere below the remote summit of Mt. Garfield, on the path between Greenleaf and Galehead Appalachian Mountain Club alpine huts, my father had had enough. "Where's the damn hut!" he exclaimed, on the steepest, boulder-studded portion of the trail. In all fairness, it was raining sideways, the wind was howling, and the blisters from new hiking boots were festering. The only photo suggests my brother and I were having fun. It was also the only time I recall my father using even a mild profanity. He was exhausted. I was exhilarated by the wild weather and rugged terrain. We cut the four-day trip short and hiked out the next day. Two years later, I went back to the mountains—on my own, crossing a new boundary wall.

In a few years, hiking became a year-round activity. Every weekend found me in the White Mountains summiting peak after peak, regardless of weather—the presidential range ridges and Dry River valley; Franconia Ridge; the vestigial logging railroad beds of Zealand Valley. In the winter of 1976, some college pals and I bushwhacked up to Garfield, in waist-deep snow, from a trail in the Pemigewasset wilderness. In the summer of 1978, I slept in the abandoned concrete fire tower base on the exposed summit of Garfield, the moon rising over the same wilderness. Another favorite night spent in those mountains was sleeping alone in Guyot shelter, the most remote in the AMC system. It was autumn and an epic electrical storm descended on the ridge above. The gods were angry. I was cozy, rattled, and content.

In time, the White Mountains were followed by the Cairngorms and Scottish Highlands—Glen Coe, Ben Nevis (even slogging up the tourist route of switchbacks in fog and cold rain was a pleasure), and Glen Affric in the Western Highlands. And each successive path remains vivid, textural, and deeply embedded in the mists of my heart as that first third grade venture into the Big Woods. Even my current path out back of our Maine home, meandering through spruce and fir to an old farm field, triggers a memory each time I walk it. *That would make a good redoubt,* I think, passing the glacial erratic. I have my knife. I have my heart communing between paths past and present. I'm gathering pine sap to keep this torch alive. A familiar path can be different every time, while this pathfinder can follow it, still age eight, on a good day.

À la recherche des voitures perdu

MY DAD WAS NOT A CAR GUY. He didn't particularly love buying or owning cars; didn't faithfully change the oil or spend precious time on washing and waxing. Cars were utilitarian transportation, not identity symbols. However, there was one car that stood out in the long line of family automotive history. It was a watershed moment, as I look back on it, having an effect beyond the automotive. It was the objective correlative of an internal shift in my father that I am still deciphering.

Something got ahold of Dad in 1968, around the onset of *Sergeant Pepper* in my world. Previously, the red Buick Skylark had been perfectly fine for commuting to work. The Dodge Polaris, a virtual aircraft carrier of a car, sufficed for family conveyance. And they followed a string of Ford Falcons when we were still a one-car family. In hindsight, I divide Nelson automotive history into Before and After the Peugeot.

That year, Dad brought home a white, four-door Peugeot 404 sedan. I remember his glow, spouting unfamiliar terms for automobile design, accessories, and driving. He pored over the owner's manual. It was French. It had a bodacious body leading toward the headlights, quasi-fins for taillights, and a diminutive hood and trunk. It was compact and solid compared to the exor-bitantly oversized American sedans of the era. The doors closed with a *basso profundo* "thunk." It had our first FM radio. He had bidden adieu to Detroit. Dad was Monsieur Hulot. We began a holiday from which we have yet to return.

"It has rack and pinion steering, and disc brakes," Dad explained, and regaled us with a verbal exposition of the engi-neering marvels. "It's better on the curves." He had never taken the time to champion any particular feature of our prior cars. Clearly, a sales pitch had beguiled him. The 404 was comfort-able, fun to drive (a new concept!), and had a lion rampant for its corporate logo. Heraldry in automobile branding, and a company that predated the automotive industry? Wow. Armand Peugeot built his family's first attempt at a car (steam, unreliable) in 1889. They had been making hand tools, kitchen equipment, and bicycles heretofore. I too was beguiled, once I learned the correct pronunciation. We now owned *une voiture*. The last time a car purchase had been a defining family moment was probably when my great grandfather purchased a Ford Model A, circa 1910.

Just like that, we were done with bench seats in the front. The Peugeot had an armrest that opened into an inter-seat storage cubby. And leather! Red. Individual seat adjustments, forward and back. *This will be my first car when I get my license . . . five years hence,* I thought. Until then, I would drive it forward and backward on our 50-foot driveway, or surreptitiously down the dirt roads in New Hampshire. Did anyone notice the car keys were missing? Where were the grown-ups anyway?

Even from my vantage point in the passenger seat, it was clear that the driving experience had become *nouveau*. Dad com-muted by car about 35 miles a day round-trip, half on wind-ing roads, half on turnpike. He now loved the feel of rounding curves on those country lanes and relished a certain mountain road in New Hampshire where he would hug the hairpin curves going downhill without touching the brakes. Dad liked it so much, he bought a red station wagon model. We became a *deux* Peugeot family.

More than an upgrade, this was a departure. It was not the exotic cars of our friends—not the Triumph TR6 my friend's dad drove, nor the neighbor's Jaguar XKE. It was certainly not the midlife muscle car. It was not a move up to fancier Buicks, or midcareer promotion to luxury American models. It was a sequel to a set of wheels with narrative potential, descriptive allure, an accent, and foreign design standards and aesthetics. After all, this car had Michelin *pneus radial*, whatever they were—another talking point. I cannot speak to the 404's full engineering prowess, maintenance record, or comparative pricing adjusted for time, but the number of 1950s and 1960s Peugeots still on the road in Africa and Cuba speaks volumes.

Then came another surprise piece of European engineering: Swedish audio components. A Bang and Olufsen stereo, turntable, and Klipsch speakers mysteriously appeared in the living room. *Sergeant Pepper* became deeper, more complex, and exponentially louder. My head spun. This automotive-audio nexus was a sea change. I began to think there was more going on. But what?

Two foreign objects had cracked open an alternate universe: Europe. Each was a first crush, and I too was smitten with these new sensory experiences and designs. I saw cars, high fidelity, and my father, in a new light. Dad's Peugeot had me at rack and pinion steering—or, *direction a crémaillère*. But it is Dad's delight in fresh discovery, "disturbing the universe," that I'm still driving, as if it's a white Peugeot 404 sedan. Now, about that XKE. . . .

Aural Postcards
from a Lake
in Maine

ITS NAME ALONE SOUNDS LIKE whispering wind and waves lapping at rocky shores: West Grand Lake. No wonder then that after three days of paddling its coves and bays in August, sleeping on a slender island where blueberries grew in bunches like grapes, it is sounds which best carry my memories of this place. Anyone can leave with a scenic view of a wilderness lake—and we did, snapping the regulation photos—but I am struck by how much more is stocked in my imagination by the auditory snapshots.

The day we set out from Farm Cove Dam, I remember the first moments of the trip as sound signatures: the thumping of tent and sleeping bags and food box being dropped into the canoe, afloat in shallow water; the coaxing of Gus, the big black dog, into his berth between thwarts; the rattling push off from the graveled shore and silky glide over weeds into the channel, coasting past the spillway.

With the first few strokes of our paddles we thumped the gunwales like timpani, but then, in the interest of hearing what else was occurring on the lake, we dampened our noise—even talking starts to seem intrusive—and focused on receiving only. Such a day, on a big sparsely inhabited Maine lake, visual details seem static, wind and wave changing imperceptibly against the backdrop of stolid green forest and unlimited sky. But the details, the excitement to be discovered in the scene, are aural: we are notified of changes in appearance by the sudden arrival of new sounds.

Things occur as sounds before they occur as sights. Something splashes a few yards to starboard. A fish jumping? An Otter? A Turtle? Missed seeing it. Some things, never sighted, are filed away as unincorporated sounds, like the numbered townships charted across this wilderness quadrant of the state never characterized with a true name.

As we slowly sweep from small cove to intermediate bay and finally to the lake at large, heading for an island camp, exiting the lee of the forested shore, the wind makes a new sign on the water, piquing the waves into a ribbony chop that chatters against the side of our boat. Gus stretches, tilting us precariously, and our paddle handles drum hard against the gunwales as we hastily grip to restore balance. Loons wail. Too far off for us to see them, they are transponders of our progress. I hear a hummingbird zoom by, hundreds of yards from shore, dipping a shoulder to eye this yellow canoe with big black dog, but hardly deviating from his flight path toward another small island. Would he conceive of his route "as the crow flies?" At noon, a bald eagle circles soundlessly on a thermal updraft above us.

The lake pools sounds from its far shores and funnels them to our ears floating midlake, carrying and magnifying brief cries, steady calls, and mechanical overtones over miles of water: from the North a small outboard engine purrs, too distant to be seen; to the West, a dog barks from a shoreline camp we cannot distinguish; thousands of feet above us, a jet's arcing contrails lead away from its plume of searing sound. Our hearing extends further than does our sight, when we are placed in a landscape of such exaggerated scale. How nearsighted we are; how far-hearinged we can become, given retraining.

As we bump between boulders landing at our island destination, a pair of crows heralds our arrival; there's no sneaking into the scene now, as their calls echo shrilly from the spruce spires. They cast off from their perch and swoop away, cavorting on the light gusts that shiver through the poplars at the water's edge. And then the red squirrels commenced their discourse on the nature of this big black dog splashing ashore from the yellow canoe. A 48-hour discourse, as it turned out, which left Gus sleep deprived and frustrated, scolded from limb to limb and from one end of the island to the other, as he panted beneath their perches. All night long we listen to his feet padding along on the pine needles or scurrying on the granite outcroppings outside our tent as he chases his frustrating quarry; and to the rain fly on the tent luffing around us, like wavelets.

For two nights, a strict sonic sequence prevailed. The din of cookstove and clanging pots sputtered out at dusk. The sun went down and the wind ceased its whispering; the crescent moon presided for a few hours over the intermediate sleepy talk of boulders soaking up the last laps of waves; and then silence deeper than starlight. Now "the ears of my ears are awake" wrote e.e. cummings. It takes the absence of sound to be this aware of hearing. No longer listening for sounds, we simply listen to—anticipating nothing, but open to anything which speaks up within range.

I recall a line from Wallace Stevens. In "The Snow Man" he writes of

> *the listener, who listens in the snow,*
> *And, nothing himself, beholds*
> *Nothing that is not there and the nothing that is.*

Little by little the background tapestry of noise has yielded, including the sounds which I brought to this island, gradually pared away to leave a secret hearing blind that I now share with squirrel and crow and loon: looking out from silence, becoming a denizen listener as if (brief impostor!) *of* this place, listening *as* this place, *to* this place.

A Return to Dunnottar Castle

AS I THINK BACK, while visiting Dunnottar Castle for the second time a few years ago, my grandfather was the living link to the old country. Not because he was born there—he was the second generation born in the new country—nor because he had visited. He hadn't. It was because he grew up hearing his grandmother's Glasgow accent—the sound of the old country.

Jeannie Callum Nelson was the matriarch, cared for by her children and grandchildren every Sunday, assuring she had coal and comfort. One of my favorite old family photos shows my father as a toddler on her knees, his father and grandfather sharing the moment in the backyard of a house in Tonawanda, New York—the new country—labeled, simply, "four generations."

My children have a "four generations" photo, in our backyard in Massachusetts: my grandfather seated at the center, my father, me, and Ariel, Spencer, and Hilary. Our first visit to Dunnottar Castle was a few years behind for me and granddad; it was still many years ahead for me and Ariel. The photo is poised between visits.

I was the fourth generation born in the United States and the first Nelson to return to the old country. In 1977, several weeks before flying home to get married, after a year spent at Stirling University, my grandfather met me in Scotland—his first trip out of the country; his only trip back.

We visited the registry of civil records in Edinburgh, where we located the leather-bound volume in which Jeannie's marriage to Alexander Nelson was recorded—written in an antique script, with all the right family names, witnesses, addresses, and clergy. It was a full-circle moment for us both, though it would be many years before I comprehended it as such. Now I can view the same exact page on the Internet. It's not the same, though. Being there at grandad's side, holding the old book, is the true experience.

One day that week, we took a bus tour. It went to Balmoral and Aberdeen and to Dunnottar Castle, a fantastic stone ruin atop the pudding stone headlands south of Aberdeen. It was ancestral home to Sir Robert de Keith in 1314, First Earl Marischal, and bears all the scars of Scottish history—Viking invaders, royal visits (Mary Queen of Scots, James VI), fires and assaults, convictions, and dereliction. It was saved from total ruin in 1925 by the First Vicountess, Lady Cowdray. The Marischal line ended after the 10th earl, George Keith, died without an heir. These stones exude Scottish history.

Perched hundreds of feet above cruel rocks, buttressed against waves and invaders, Dunnottar is a castle you would rather defend than attack. It is a fortress . . . with cozy parlors and a dance hall. It has its own bakery, and brewery, using the cistern in the courtyard to obtain safe drinking water.

In September, I got to revisit, retracing with my daughter the steps up the fortified stairway that my grandfather and I had trod. She was now the student in Scotland, having just completed a graduate degree, and I had become the living link to my grandfather. Boucle bouclé, is the term the French use for this arc of connective stories. In her master's degree thesis, Ariel calls it "narrative cartography."

I came bearing a few pebbles—circle rocks—from our Maine beach, an offering to the stones of Dunnottar from a world away; from the shores where our family arc had deposited us over those four generations. Ariel and I each tossed a pebble from the window of the castle keep onto the cliffs. And a jar of pebbles from the cove at Dunnottar sits on my mantle back in Maine, emblems of our intergenerational and geographical journeys—one and the same thing, when it comes to the old country.

Dunnottar made an impression on me, lo these 42 years hence—its stone steps that generations have trod; that I have trod with the generations; the windows looking Viking-ward on the North Sea and on hayfields to the west; its aura of stolid power and protection, endurance and isolation.

And I ponder our own actual family "castle," the wee stone cottage in the village of Spott, west of Dunbar, where grandfather's great grandfather was a plowman. They never met. There are no photos of our family there, alas, but it still stands; is inhabited; awaiting a visit. Next trip. With fresh pebbles to exchange. I'd just like to set my foot on the stone stoop that generations have trod.

When Clotheslines Last in the Dooryard Bloom'd

SURELY THERE IS A CLOTHESLINE EQUINOX, the boundary line between indoor and outdoor laundry drying, when an ecstatic bloom of myriad garments takes place in the local dooryards. Alas, it used to be the sole way to dry. Now, it seems like the outlier.

Bring back the clothesline. It is more than the sum of its simple parts.

My wife loves a clothesline. "It says, 'Someone's home.'" It flies the flags of the homeowner, indicating residence, like a baronial pennant.

She's not alone. "I counted eight, one for each day of the week," said another clothesline aficionado, of her neighbor's colorful shirts. "One security shirt and one for current wear. Planned like a true engineer."

A clothesline flies the flags of order, intention, and purpose too. A clothesline exhibits a homeowner's strategy. Shirts and pants hung out to dry practically fold and crease themselves.

Surely Thoreau would appreciate the economy in that, like the firewood maxim attributed to him: My logs warmed me twice, "once while I was splitting them, and again when they were on the fire."

The clothesline has a graphic allure. My wife's favorite paintings in any medium are clotheslines. Perhaps even in their static, two-dimensional state, they inevitably suggest motion, wind power, and the alchemy of evaporation. And they have that horizon line that draws our vision far into the side yard frame.

A walk around town would aid the discussion, except fewer and fewer clotheslines survive. Doesn't everyone know that good clotheslines make good neighbors? I won't comment on your tighty-whiteys; you lay off my bleach accidents and long johns. We're lettin' it all hang out. Our unmentionables are airing out properly, roaming for a few hours in the sun.

And there is nothing like clean sheets, spinnakering in the breeze for an afternoon before battening down the mattress for a fragrant sleep. Clotheslines are backyard schooners, four sheets to the wind.

There must certainly be an equation to describe the air-dry, latent energy conservation coefficient of the clothesline at work (or is it at rest?) on a summer day in coastal Maine—after mowing the lawn? Inquiring minds want to know what the carbon offsets are for a week's worth of, say, flannel shirts, hung with regulation clothespins, arms below, shirttails above, one morning in Maine. What is the drying time, divided by number of shirts, length of line, temperature, and relative humidity, versus an equivalent bundle of shirts in a gas or electric dryer? Onshore or off-shore breezes? How is drying time affected by wind speed? Fabric must also be a consideration. Cotton, wool, polyester; a blend? Surely this too affects drying.

Fortunately, we have the Paul Manning Line-Dry Curve. It synthesizes all these values: fabric, wind strength and direction, temperature, humidity and even line tension and length—a thorough assimilation of all the complex variables. The conclusion is clear: line dry your clothes. The carbon offsets are inestimable.

How about the emotional offsets? What the PMLDC does not—indeed, cannot—account for is an aesthetic appreciation of the dooryard clothesline. For how could one scientifically account for what is an ecstatic emotional response to the fragrance, say, of a sundried flannel shirt? Sheets perfumed by adjacent lilacs? The loft of cotton pillow cases lovingly tussled dry near a spruce grove? *To sleep, perchance to dream.*

Mermaids We
Have Heard
on High

A CHRISTMAS TREE is a miscellany of childhoods, of geographic locations, of extended clan development, and seasonal whimsy. It is an archive of ornaments from school art projects and homespun crafts—some with fingerprints still intact, and glitter and hot glue dripping from popsicle sticks or paper strips on hand-glued ornaments. And it is a display of generations-worth of sacred objects and hand-me-downs. It is a re-enactment of rituals of retrieval, decoration, addition, and storage. It is vernacular Christmas ornaments and mementos of time and place. It is family archeology.

At my house, the tree goes up and out they come: the cookie-cutter ornaments made of salt dough and embedded sparkles, now decades into their eventual decay into crumbs. The half-life of salt dough may be eons. No one has ever seen the final decay.

There are miniature Amish quilts, Hilary's second-grade Guatemalan "God's Eyes." Ariel's ceramic birds seem to be enduring quite well. There are school photos pasted on cardboard—Spencer missing his front teeth; me, in high school, reclining on a motorcycle—assuming their place of honor on each new year's tree. And lights—ring upon ring of lights. Sometimes, we've found, there's even a stowaway from the forest where we harvested the tree: a bird's nest secreted among the branches. Bonus ornament. The wild things participate in the miscellany. They all become heirlooms in the making.

Though some years angels and stars have adorned the treetop, this is the year of the mermaid, thanks to a creative friend who imagined repurposing plastic masks. Add sparkles and sequins and a little paint and voila. "[Mermaids] we have heard on high, Sweetly singing o'er the plains." Who is to say a siren cannot top a Christmas tree, especially in our seacoast town? T.S. Eliot would approve. "I have heard the mermaids singing, each to each," he wrote, then lamented, "I do not think they'll sing to me." Their unheard melodies do lure the eye upward. They preside over the living room, as the incoming tide of presents washes around the base of the tree. Can the three wise lobstermen, traveling from down east, be far behind? Naturally, we have a lobster trap ornament. It's an epiphany for sure: Merangels!

Each year we cut a section from the tree base before securing it in the stand. We count the rings and inscribe a note as to who fetched it from the woods. Last year's tree "cookie" had eleven rings and we imagined where we lived when it began its journey toward the place of honor in our house and hearts this year. Annual rings, a chain of ornaments handing off from tree to tree, Christmas to Christmas, child to teenager to adult, like the annual rings of family itself. Here is the inscription on the tree cookie from 2003: "Hilary, Ariel, and Dad cut this down. December 14, 2004." It dangles now from an upper branch on Tree 2017, and we can think about what it was doing back in 2004. And next year this year's "cookie" of annual rings will be hanging up there beside it, as the traditions continue.

My Band of Brothers

WHAT MAKES HAPPY PEOPLE? Having friends, social connections, interactions between people with commonality. As E.M. Forster wrote, "Only connect."

David Brooks says, "A lot of the important skills are day-to-day communications skills: throwing the conversation back and forth without interrupting, adding something meaningful to what the other person just said, telling jokes, reminiscing about the past, anticipating how the other person might react to your comment so you can frame it in a way that's most helpful."

I realized my good fortune having pals that text me every day: my best buddies from high school—long ago and far away. These rock and roll band mates from London, 1972, Marc and Jeff, remain stalwarts for daily conversation about music, politics, and our youthful memories and diversions. Despite very divergent paths in later life, we're still connected to our youths. We have things in common. Still.

We were a band of American teenagers in London, thanks to our fathers' careers, and attending the same school. More importantly, Marc, Jeff, and I were devoted to the same vibrant rock music scene. Though from different backgrounds of the United

States, in truth we hailed from our affection for the rock and roll we witnessed in the concert halls of the great city. As bandmates we had a deep affinity.

Our best memories coalesce around Royal Albert Hall. Jeff and Marc can regale with memories of Cream's farewell concert, Jimi Hendrix, and Led Zeppelin. We all saw The Band, Yes, Jethro Tull, Iron Butterfly. Add outdoor concerts in Hyde Park with The Rolling Stones, Humble Pie, or Grand Funk Railroad. I was in the front row when Johnny Winter played a surprise encore with Traffic. Name any ascendant band of the era—we were there. We remember. We connect.

We'll always have the day Jeff and I strolled past Crosby, Stills, and Nash looking disoriented in the silver department at Harrod's, or happened to be at the Hard Rock Café when the Grateful Dead came in to be seated at the large round table by the front door. We tried not to be obnoxious while trolling for tickets to that night's concert. Saw Jackson Browne with Joni Mitchell on another occasion. Rock stars gotta eat. Or the day Marc returned from summer vacation back home in the states with a new Gibson Fire Bird guitar and a Fender Bassman amp. It went to 11.

We were trying to *be* rockers; to sound like our idols; to adore a band or song and put effort into imitation. We might as well have been a Crosby, Stills, Nash and Young/Buffalo Springfield tribute band, whose songs we played at Friday night basement band practice and high school dances.

We were dispersed by parental job transfers and graduations. Sure, there was a 20-year hiatus while we went to college, married, had families, and developed careers. Then an accidental reunion occurred. I was dining at the Lucky Platter in Evanston, Illinois in 1996 when Jeff walked in. Instant recognition. We picked up where we left off . . . just as we do every day today;

just as we did every day in 1972 at school, and Saturday nights at band practice.

Technology that didn't exist in our youth helps—updates on singer songwriters of our vintage, new album releases, and, sadly, lots of obituaries (increasingly frequent) for our favorite rockers. Jeff just texted: "Keef is on Sunday Morning!" Last week: "The best albums turning 50 this year." Our vintage! Can Neil Young's *Harvest* truly be that old? Yes. We were covering his tunes when we were 16. Do the math. I conjure the album cover with a pang.

Marc keeps tabs on the BBC, sharing articles of interest from Royals to rockers and curiosities of British life developed during his many school years in London—uniquely British stories to tweak nostalgia. He also curates an Instagram account devoted to classic rock guitar players. I curate political cartoons. Jeff keeps in touch with Soho London guitar shop mavens. We have discovered emojis. We laugh at the same, sometimes juvenile, things. We can complete each other's sentences, especially if they are song lyrics. Next to my brother, they are my oldest friends.

Though dispersed coast-to-coast; retired geezers; the world of memory has never retired. It's flat and asynchronous. We each continue to inhabit London, 1970s, and travel back and forth from present to past. And such rich, ongoing friendships are a good remedy for isolation and loneliness. Or is it the music? As Jack Black says in *School of Rock,* "I pledge allegiance to the band." Time for a 50th anniversary reunion tour. It's good to be in a band. Just like Keef.

Lefty Fourchette,
cuisinière

*There are two schools of good writing about food:
the mock-epic and the mystical microcosmic.*

—Adam Gopnik

LEFTY FOURCHETTE EST DANS SA CUISINE creating her *prix fixe, table d'hôte,* holiday menu. It promises gustatory revelations. De rigeuer. Comme d'habitude, for the wee future Michelin chef, though she eschews the customary toque. She's working on her fine dining motor skills, measuring her meals with plastic spoons. She is veritably on top of the stove. And she's giving her family a sneak peek by hosting a special tasting—all just 20 months into her cordon bleu schooling. Reservations are going fast.

Ever since she moved into her petite practice kitchen, she's been working on sauces (Bechamel, Meuniere, des Tomates), roulades, sundry amuse-bouche, hors d'oeuvres, pasta, crème caramel, and Proustian madeleines. The madeleines especially are just as one remembers. Buche de noel could be on the holiday menu too! La bouche de Lefty is an infallible guide to delight.

Someday she will be able to say these words and order off an *à la carte* menu. For now, "umami" is her favorite word and she repeats it all day long like a mantra. Or is it "yo, mama?" Sometimes her pronunciation is difficult to understand, as when she is twirling her pasta between mouthfuls. We just say, "Yes, chef!"

Lefty sandwiches her culinary efforts between a busy schedule of naps, episodes of Bluey and The Great British Baking Show, and stints at her favorite playground. Then there is her staff to train: Juanita, BB, Papito, and Maman. Before service each day, she must review the menu and assign tasks to the sous chefs and even the plongeurs—Fox, Bluey, and Mango—though Lefty is not above loading the dishwasher herself, for the kitchen is her domain and she rules over all tasks.

From early on it was clear that Lefty savors food. Period. Her customary petite dejeuner of fruit, "pancakies" (crépes) or waffles (gaufres), and yogurt was a tasting menu giving her ideas for *les plats du jour*. As she carefully selects blueberries or banana slices, one by one, daintily bringing them to her mouth between thumb and forefinger, her focus and concentration are intense. Each mouthful is considered with careful thought and savor; each ingredient with appreciation. She cleanses her palate between tastes with a soupçon of *jus de pomme* in her personal sippy cup. Juanita, her kitty sous-chef, delights in the crumbs that fall from the prep area, particularly crumbs of *tartine Fourchette grillé au beurre*.

Lefty selects only the best of ingredients—the freshest, organic fruits and vegetables—and is fortunate to live within range of a host of organic growers. She shops daily, cruising the aisles of l'épicerie, taking samples and testing the fruits and vegetables for ripeness. On to the cheese aisle! Bread, muffins, bagels . . . the shopping cart fills and excitement for the dejeuner builds.

The young chef comes from a family with a long line of cooks. Her mother and aunt were pastry chefs from an early age, taught at the elbow of their great grandmother, Evelyn, and her recipes from the Old Country. Another great grandmother won many prizes for her baking. Her Jell-O mold salad was also legendary. Lefty's uncle is a famous barbecue pitmaster and saucier, trained in Chicago. Her grandfather is a boulanger Mainois. Specialité: brioche. Even her great and great great grandfathers, on her mother's father's side, were known for casseroles, sauces, and pies. Cuisine is in her DNA. Extending the family tradition is a given; her mantle. She has had greatness thrust upon her. Can a *tarte aux poires Fourchette* be far behind in the pantheon of baking recettes? Non!

Ah, childhood, observed by food writers through the eyes of an emerging culinary talent! Each day is a unique pantry of fresh tastes and smells; every day a new experience. Time was, we all embraced the new day as Lefty does—every novel food introduced was a discovery; a taste revelation; a fresh inspiration. Now her *plats du jour* are trips in memory back to our own gastronomic inductions. We see each meal through the eyes of the young chef and thereby rediscover our own apprenticeship at the table of maman, when the morning stars sang together. Ah! Here comes the Bechamel . . . on fresh pasta, aux courgettes! Nummy. And le dessert? Maman never fails to provide.

Putting the
Year to Bed

WE HAD A BUMPER CROP of acorns this year, plumped by abundant water and warmth. Sitting in the driveway in October, I felt bombarded by oak hail on even windless days as they pelted the roof of our Subaru—and me, hard hat required. Clever oaks, letting go of their leaves and seeding the next forest at the same time. I'll spend the coming cold months detecting where the mice have stashed them, not just in the woodpile, but in my car's cabin air filter, various pockets in the engine cavity, and even the spare tire well, just like last year. The mice put the year to bed by turning my car into their pantry. When I start it up, acorns rattle under the hood and across the interior of the dashboard when I take the first corner. I fully expect an oak sapling will sprout from my driver's side heating duct by May.

I filled a Mason jar with acorns. Now I'm forcing them to sprout in a special vase. The acorn nestles in a little cup atop and is encouraged to send its roots down into the vase. It is. Eventually a tree shoot goes upward, then leafs out and prepares for spring transplanting. This year's acorns will be next year's saplings. I envision a row of young oaks out front to complement the older ones I've been favoring among the fir and spruce to make climbing trees for my granddaughter with evenly-spaced limbs and room for perching, and some year a tree house.

Birdsongs wane. The summer songsters are long gone—the bluebirds stayed the longest—but the owls are always here, watching and awaiting. One night, a familiar barred owl spent quite a long time sitting on an oak branch surveying open ground below. My game camera caught him. He preened, looked around, flew off, returned, perhaps consumed a mouse out of camera range, then spread his wings and was gone. I hear him most nights calling across the field to his hunting partners. He is selective about his camera candids.

I've watched the deer since spring as their coats redden, then shed, then darken again for winter camouflage and solar absorption. A doe and three yearlings and an eight-point buck have been enjoying the drops from my two ancient apple trees that bear fruit every other year. They visit most nights and my game camera catches the buck in action, browsing the ground, chewing, taking his time; bulking up. My French friend sees the photos and suggests I am feeding him so he'll feed me. "Tu le laisses manger, s'engraisser et ensuite tu le mange," writes Jean, who raises sheep, "Avec une petite sauce au Jurançon,—" his favorite vintage of the Béarn region. However, I hunt only with the camera, though I don't begrudge someone else the shot at food. Pick-up trucks with gun racks park on the forest verge, no doubt scouting a suitable deer stand, tracking, ready for the season to open, as the days cool and shorten. We don our safety orange hats and coats.

It is pie weather. Fruitcake weather follows. The shortest day, the last day of the solar year, is still to come, but I'm thinking even farther ahead to how soon the days begin to lengthen again. The light is never static. Susan Cooper knows this tipping point:

All the long echoes sing the same delight,
This shortest day,
As promise wakens in the sleeping land;

In mid-October, I refilled the oil tank, having held out for as long as possible. The invoice confirms how much fuel I used last year—a thrifty 144 gallons. I am ready to spend it in the months ahead . . . but not just yet. I'd rather wear another sweater and a hat. The annual two cords of firewood are stashed under cover where it can dry a final time; within easy reach of the wood stove. Fred came and cleaned the chimney. Between furnace, wood stove, and sunshine through the front windows we will be warm. Get out the down comforters. Add dog. Enough. Summer and now autumn have been put to bed as we move indoors. The sun's wick is turned down lower and lower with each dusk. All us denizens are perching, foraging, stashing, fattening, and waiting—the verbs of December—for the new year days to lengthen and awaken a new go-round. For now, we bears are preparing to sleep, to awaken when the maple trees promise sugar.

Where the Unicorns Sing

THE DAY BEGINS EARLY, with Freya June. First light. The sun has yet to fully rise. The howler monkeys are hardly stirring. And yet, with her eyes barely open, Freya June is focused and hard at work. The world will not wait. Let's get busy.

"Guess what? I found my lovey (her stuffed sloth, Mango) all by myself! Why are the birds yelling? I think they're telling their mommies that they're early . . . "—all before her mama has had a chance to inhale much less make coffee.

Working her imagination downward from the tree canopy to life on the rainforest floor, Freya June is wondering about other animals. "Why do animals have whiskers? Why do cats jump so high? Does Jackson miss his mommy?"

Jackson is not a cat. He is her best human friend. He attended her third birthday party back in the spring. The theme was unicorns, her favorite animal.

And then, shifting gears: "I could dream all over the place plobably. Mommy, am I three? Am I gonna be four? Why can't I be five and then four?" Has she been listening to "My back pages" by Nobel Laureate Bob Dylan?—"I was so much older then, I'm younger than that now"—Or should I be writing about quantum entanglement?

Animal physiology, empathy for friends, and ergonomics, dream and number theory get the day rolling while I too am still grinding coffee beans and putting bananas on my oatmeal. All before 06:00 central time. The day holds such immense promise.

This is a developmental advance on the prior "why?" phase. Now, questions require precise, not general, answers. Dare I use the word "intellectual" pursuits? Her mind is in high gear. Every day is another exploration in several dimensions of the known universe.

Much of the rest of the day will involve unicorns. Unicorns on the *playa Manzanita*, unicorns in the swimming pool, unicorns for Halloween costumes. If there were unicorn ice cream cones, Freya would be enjoying them and her chin would be covered with unicorn sprinkles. Chocolate will suffice.

I have taken to sending her a daily "unicorn song." She has decided that my bagpipes play "unicorn music"—so be it, the mystical creature being the emblem of Scotland, after all. And so, I record a real bagpipe tune with a fanciful title to magically send through the ether to Freya. "I call this tune, 'The Unicorn walking over the hill to the mailbox.'" Or, "Here's one called 'The Unicorn swimming in the swimming pool with Freya.'" Yesterday, "The Unicorn choosing a Halloween costume" was the song of the day. I follow the Scottish naming pattern for *ceol beag*, the small music of the pipes, giving a march or strathspey connection to a person, event, or landscape. "Oft in the Stille night" deserves to be "Oft in the Stille Night the Unicorn took a walk." "Colonel Macleod" has been awaiting renaming: "Colonel Macleod rides his Unicorn to the Playa." He has been seeking suitable transportation. You're welcome, Colonel.

For Halloween, Freya eventually settled on being a butterfly princess for the school assembly. Last year, her first real Halloween dress-up, she was Kamala Harris, right down to the Chuck Converse All Star sneakers. Her parents accompanied her as a Secret Service detail, talking into their sleeves and wearing sunglasses. They even posed next to a big black SUV. This year: no Secret Service.

The tune du jour was "The Unicorn dancing on the playa with the Butterfly Princess," a nice lilting strathspey. But I stand corrected.

"Unicorns don't go on the playa," Freya informed me. And her mother added, "She may be losing interest in unicorns." I guess it's tough to compete with the exotic flora and fauna of their surroundings, and it's time to move ahead to the next fascination. She has been wondering why monkeys have thumbs like hers. New tune: "The monkeys of Loch Lomond," by the piper with opposable thumbs.

They were headed to the beach to watch the sunset and explore tide pools for hermit crabs, or climb driftwood, another favorite pastime.

"It never gets old," Hilary says, of the sunset spectacle. The playa is on the Pacific coast of Costa Rica, which looks like a perfect setting for unicorn rides on the sand, in my humble opinion. In fact, "I have heard the [unicorns] singing, each to each." I shall wear my trousers rolled and put a unicorn atop my Christmas tree.

Knitting Up
the Raveled
Sleeve of Care

I ASSOCIATE KNITTING WITH THE FACULTY MEETINGS of yore. French teacher Jeannie Cooperman had hands like a basketball player and could knit baby sweaters with the smallest needles at a lightning pace during a protracted discussion of, say, recess rules. Another colleague, Vera Nordal, could knit a traditional Norwegian sweater from memory. Her husband, Oddvar, my mentor and colleague, was a former member of the Norwegian underground in World War II, a radio operator directing Allied bombers from high in the mountains. I know his code name. The kids nicknamed him Ja-Ja, due to his accent.

Vera's family, who had fled Frankfurt in the 1930s, escaped occupied France with her brother and parents by walking over the Pyrenees, then shipping from Lisbon to New York, where she learned her third language, English. She and Oddvar met in Pakistan working in refugee camps after the partition in 1949.

In this country, Oddvar would sit on an American ski lift and lament how much skiing opportunity was being missed by only skiing downhill. Looking below, he would explain the attack line of ascending tracks he would follow if skiing at home in Norway. Vera spoke English, French, German, Norwegian, and Russian. The complex syntax of a Norwegian sweater pattern was a piece of cake.

There always seems to be a favorite sweater. In 1977, a friend in Edinburgh, Robert Mitchell, gave me a very old, ornate, beautifully knitted Scottish sweater, an heirloom no doubt. I've never seen another one like it. The muscular cable stitches are a complex brocade up the front and winding up the sleeves. The collar is a high turtleneck. The wool is rich in lanolin and still sheds water, in addition to having the fragrance of highland adventures. I'm wearing it in a favorite winter mountaineering photo taken on the southwest side of Ben Nevis. It has also been to the summit of Mt. Monroe in the White Mountains, worn by my wife, Lesley. Robert said that Scottish fishing villages had their own sweater patterns that would identify the wearer's home port.

Alas, though it does not fit me any longer, it's cherished in the family. My daughter Ariel now owns the "Mitchell" sweater, plus a hand-knit Scottish cardigan purchased by Lesley in 1981. The elbows have thinned from loving wear; moths have put a dent in it. So, Ariel had its three holes invisibly rewoven by Karol Steele in Hawick, down on the Scottish borders. She added suede elbow patches and new buttons. It is in her wardrobe and it's good to see it on her. Such sweaters are meant to be worn and then handed down, with repair provenance.

In the 1980s, Lesley attempted an intricate cable-knit pattern, given her by a talented friend, and I eagerly awaited a new sweater—an echo of The Mitchell in a dark green yarn and much less lanolin. It evolved into a many-month and then multi-year project. Somehow, by the time it was finished, the size was mangled. As it turned out, it would fit Lesley, not me. Now it fits neither of us and lives in an antique blanket chest awaiting a chance with the next generation.

Lesley has knitting genes. Her mother was a sophisticated knitter and equally talented seamstress—with her own knitting store and classes, for a while.

"She was always knitting," remembers Lesley. "She had a project in every room. Always busy. No idle time. She never just sat still. She could knit with her eyes closed and always made ski sweaters for each of us for Christmas. We always knew what we were getting."

When you knit midcentury couture outfits for your daughter's Barbie dolls, you use a 0-size needle. Her trove of knitting and crocheting needles is stored in our basement awaiting interest and new hands, including size 0. Among the needles are a few unfinished projects in fragrant yarn and lost patterns and projects, probably destined to remain incomplete. Nothing Norwegian, or Scottish—a lost syntax of a gift or tribute.

Sweaters tell our stories, as memories purl.

The Land Between
the Rivers

I "WILL ARISE AND GO NOW" to the house of summer. It is the
first day warm enough to keep the windows open at night. The
outside is coming back inside with birdsong and howls. The owls
have been there all the time, of course, but I have not heard them
coming out at dusk; the rains have soaked the roof of the forest,
but the sound of droplets on their way through the leaves to the
floor is inaudible. The moon comes and goes without comment.
But now, outside air is inside. The summer house is open. We've
spent so long sheltering, holding cold and frozen precipitation at
bay, watching the log pile dwindle—now we can yield. Even the
fog, here on the Maine coast, can seep in and find welcome. We
exhale our winter selves and inhale our summer selves.

It's changeover day, as when one summer tenant departs and
the next one arrives—the house is swept of winter sounds, the
sheets are hung on the line to refresh in the sun, and the hermit thrush and vireo filter past open windows and through the
screens to delight us. They are back. Our summer selves are back.

It sends me on a pilgrimage to the summer house in the Saco
River valley—the house with the orange canoe—inhaling the
morning and evening birdsongs, the mountain water running

over pebbled streams, the maple forests, the distant freight train's weal coming down the valley from Crawford Notch, the headwaters of our river, of our summer, then and always.

We would arrive after a long drive with boats and duffle bags on the roof of the station wagon and run first to check the water level and river channel after the spring run-off. Then we fling wide the windows to air out the winter doldrums. The stairs creak—untrodden since last August. The windowsills are dusty and fly-littered. The driftwood and pebble collections of previous summers have been there sunning all winter, along with a few eagle feathers and birch bark. Let new collections begin. Driftwood mobiles! Jars of new pebbles! Pressed flowers! But first, the air exchange; the season exchange. Let summer in.

The deck was like the prow of a ship looming above the riverbank. The spinnaker of summer billowed before us, pulling us on. Weigh anchor. My bed was at the top of the A-frame, a bunkbed in the crow's nest, where I spent mornings languishing with a book before descending the steep boat ladder to begin my explorations of the woods and riverbank. There are new trees across the branch stream; the spring ice has gouged new divots in our landing; the sandy cove is migrating downstream. The river tells us the story of winter, while we were away.

Memory is a trout holding steady midstream. It awaits food, inspects floating possibilities, then, rising to a wriggling fly, leaps and swallows and finds itself wriggling on a hook. The adults were moving around outside my field of vision. The summer beckoned to the children in a different manner. But now that I am an adult, I ponder the moments of transition and transfer—from season to season, from work to play and leisure, from effort to languor, the need to be doing to the effortless floating need to be doing nothing; to be heedless. There was the quality of light—hot intensity out on the water, versus the dappled greenness of the cool woods. Or the water—snorkeling above the riverbed, submerging in the thermoclines, or trying to grab the wary trout. We held our breath as long as it took to swim down and move a big boulder, divert the stream, and make a pool.

At night, the river lulled us, murmuring, unlike the restless ocean. Without TV, we read or were read to, and heard foreign radio stations careening off the ionosphere. The mosquitos whined for entry at the screens. Moths flitted at the outside lightbulb. Crickets and tree frogs chorused. Dylan Thomas called it "holy darkness." We lit the fireplace in July. I can't remember deeper slumbers.

My favorite summer was 1969: the summer of Woodstock and driftwood mobiles. I emulated Calder with foraged materials. Using Dad's power drill and copper wire, I made elaborate aerial ballets with ice-polished sticks and weathered boards washed up by the river. Detritus turns to art. The A-frame was always the place of first experiences—swimming in fast water, hiking in the White Mountains, being alone; early romances that would echo through the rest of my life; and listening to the song of the mountain watershed.

I still reside in June 1974, after high school graduation, spending a week there with a buddy, decompressing. Two massive oaks had bridged the stream that spring. I could tightrope in my bare feet over the current and peer straight down above big trout. The memory persists. They levitated languidly midstream awaiting temptations floating past on the stream's surface: bugs, mayflies, ants, and perhaps my in-artfully presented dry fly. I could not interest him, though I flogged the stream until dusk. Catching one didn't matter. I can watch forever from my mental perch lulled by the current through time and the trout that can't be landed, waving like a memory just out of reach.

And each summer had a tipping point: the moment when you realize you are closer to departure than to arrival. It becomes a melancholy count down. The light is changing. August air hints of autumn; dread winter. Soon, the house of winter will return. Time to close up. What's inside—new memories—migrates out and away with us, back down the dirt road, until next year.

Summer is a trove of fables; of sojourns by which we measure ourselves. Is it the magical place, or magical time, the other river, skirting the happy isle of summer, filling a real place and my reinvention of it from downstream, that I'm collecting? Dipping my toes in one current tests the power of the other, as with any hallowed memory, as I sit astride the run-off-toppled trees. The summer sun always warms. The cold, cold current bearing us downstream always stabs at the heart.

About the Author

Author portrait © Michelle L. Morby

*I am an education writer, a rural writer, a local writer,
a transcendental writer like Thoreau, and a writer who
stumbles upon a good opening line and allows it to unfurl
and lead me on. Some days I scribble down an idea in my
little pocket notebook. Other days an opening line will
spring to mind as I walk, hastening me home to type it
out. The rest of the day will be spent taking dictation from
the imagination and word associations it precipitates.*

After a long career as a teacher and administrator in public
and private schools in Boston, San Francisco, Chicago, Philadelphia, and Castine, Maine, Nelson retired to write and bake
bread and the scones of destiny. His writing has appeared in

numerous periodicals, including the *Ellsworth American*, the *Castine Patriot*, *Maine Boats, Homes & Harbors*, *Bangor Daily News*, *Bangor Metro*, *Maine Times*, *Philadelphia Inquirer*, *Taproot*, *The Christian Science Monitor*, *Wooden Boat*, *Northern Journeys*, *Maine Public Radio*, *Education Week*, *Appalachia*, and the *Portland Press Herald*. He lives with his wife, Lesley Brody Nelson, in Penobscot, Maine.